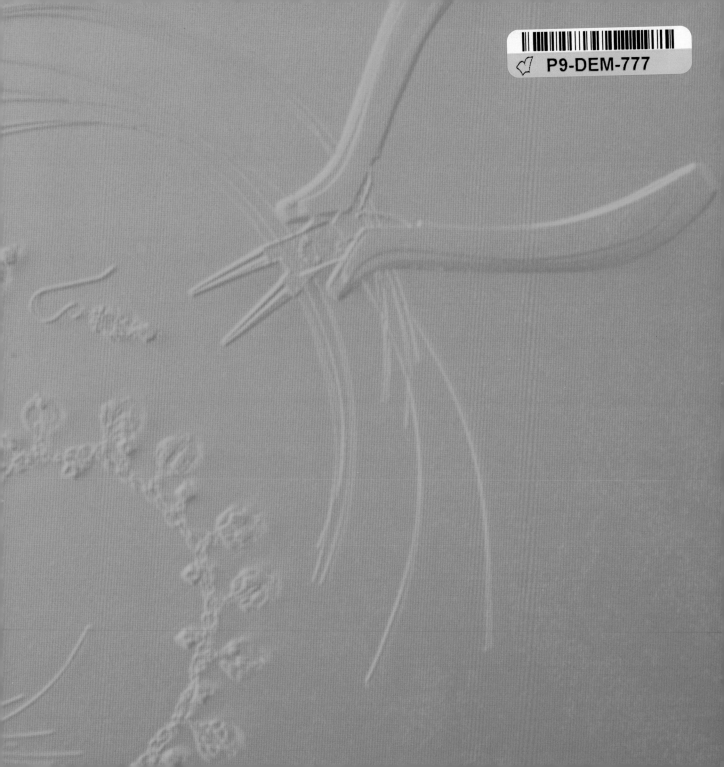

GETTING **STARTED**
making
wire
jewelry
and more

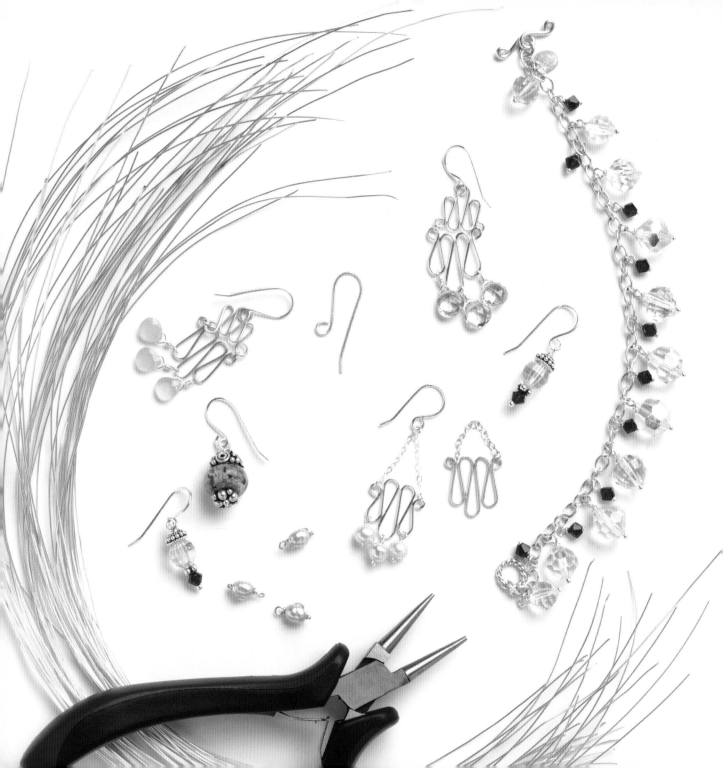

GETTING **STARTED**

making
wire
jewelry
and more

Linda**Chandler** and
Christine**Ritchey**

INTERWEAVE.
interweavestore.com

Photography: Joe Coca, Lloyd Ritchey, and Linda Chandler
Photo styling: Paulette Livers
Cover and interior design: Paulette Livers

Interweave Press LLC
201 East Fourth Street
Loveland, CO 80537-5655 USA
interweavestore.com

Printed in China by C & C Offset Printing Co., Ltd.

Library of Congress Cataloging-in-Publication Data

Chandler, Linda L., 1946-
  Getting started making wire jewelry and more / Linda L. Chandler, Christine R. Ritchey.
      p. cm.
  Includes index.
  ISBN 978-1-931499-87-3 (hbk.)
  1. Jewelry making. 2. Wire craft. I. Ritchey, Christine R., 1951- II. Title.
  TT212.C452 2005
  745.594'2--dc22
                              2005001685

15 14 13 12 11

acknowledgments

First I thank Linda Chandler, for being so darn creative at coming up with so many original designs at a moment's notice. Also, thank you for your great process photos—even though you did melt your camera! I am so fortunate to work with a lady who is so tremendously talented. Neither *Getting Started Making Wire Jewelry* nor *Woven Wire Jewelry* would exist without Linda, and that would be a darn shame.

Thanks to everyone at Interweave Press for doing such a great job on this book: Betsy Armstrong for encouragement, solace, humor, and friendship; Judith Durant for her amazing editing skills and hysterically funny comments; Christine Townsend for being my sounding board and friend-in-need, and to Phoenix for making her happy; Paulette Livers for her incredible talent in book layout and making us look so pretty. Also, to Rebecca Campbell for wading bravely into a work-in-progress. These books are truly a team effort.

I thank all you wonderful readers of *Woven Wire Jewelry*, our first book, for the e-mails, letters, and positive feedback. I feel I have made some true friends and have enjoyed our conversations. You are the reason these books are such a labor of love and why Linda and I keep writing them.

Last, but always first in my heart, I thank Lloyd Ritchey, my wonderful husband who is always there for me. I am so lucky to have a husband who is tremendously talented at writing and photography, which always reflects in my work for the better. Your patience, talent, support—and lately, cooking—have kept me sane, productive, and well fed. You are an amazing man and I am blessed to have you as my husband. I love you.

—Christine Ritchey

There are so many people to thank for their help with *Getting Started Making Wire Jewelry*. The one person I must not forget to thank, as she was probably my most important mentor, is my high school art teacher, Ms. Sara Jinks. Some thirty-plus years ago she made me feel worthwhile by telling me I was a "genius." I think about her often, especially when people praise my work and talent. She was the one person in my young, impressionable years who gave me encouragement.

Thanks to my dedicated partner, Christine Ritchey, who works magic with words and translates my work into wonderful and understandable directions for readers to follow. Christine also takes care of the business side of creating our books and works endless hours at times, for which I am eternally grateful. Thanks, too, to Christine's husband, Lloyd Ritchey, who has been the voice of reason and Christine's motivator.

I thank my husband, Bud Chandler, who lovingly supports me in my jewelry adventures and is still making my tools, fixing ones that break, and taking care of my very spoiled bird, Bailey. I owe thanks to my son, Travis Chandler, who built my computer and keeps it up to date with the latest technology, and to my grandson, Ryan Workman, the apple of my eye. Ryan assists me constantly with my computer through his immense knowledge of computer language and software.

Many thanks to my mother, Corean Higdon, who keeps me fed and takes wonderful care of our home so that I can devote more time to creating jewelry and developing books. I'm grateful for my students and close friends who inspire me with their insight and creativity.

And, finally and especially, thanks to my wonderful daughter, Shane Rene Workman, who guides me in my work by giving me "thumbs up" or "thumbs down"—my best friend who is always here when I need her for advice, moral support, and her beautiful hands—and just doing whatever needs to be done.

—Linda Chandler

contents

introduction

Making jewelry is a lot of fun. With the right materials and tools, you can whip up a pair of earrings for a fancy occasion or a pretty bracelet for someone special. Making jewelry is really handy when you forget a birthday or other significant occasion!

Jewelry making can be very empowering. Perhaps you've seen a piece of jewelry and admired it, but there's something about it that you didn't like. By making the piece yourself, you can have exactly what you want. Color, bead/stone, and size can be changed to fit your wishes.

One of the most rewarding things about making jewelry is giving it to others. There's a huge amount of satisfaction in seeing someone wearing jewelry you have made, looking great, and loving it. The sight will make you smile every time.

Making jewelry can also supplement your income. There are crafts shows, galleries, shops, boutiques, and, of course, the wonderful world of the Internet—all are possible markets for your jewelry. Don't be surprised when friends and relatives offer to pay you to make something for them to wear or give away. It happens all the time!

Have fun with this book. Don't be hard on yourself if you don't make something perfectly the first time. Or even the fifth time! Everything worth learning takes practice. If you have a bunch of 5 millimeter beads lying around, and the project calls for 7 millimeter beads, don't hesitate to adjust the project to use what's on hand.

The techniques and projects presented here are guidelines. Want to use a different bead than what we used? Want to use half-hard wire instead of dead soft (see Materials and Tools on pages 4 to 5 for an explanation of these terms)? Go ahead! Use what you've got and get what you want. Let your imagination be your guide. Play and have fun!

As a hobby, jewelry making is very relaxing (most of the time!), and it's a wonderful outlet for creativity. Being able to say, "I made it myself!" is a great feeling.

Shopping

To make jewelry, you've got to have stuff to make jewelry with, so go get some stuff!

The first stop will probably be your local bead shop. Walk around the whole place and scope things out. Besides beads of every color, shape, and size, many well-stocked bead shops also carry tools, wire, and jewelry findings.

Hobby stores can be very exciting. Obviously, you'll head straight for the jewelry-making section for wire, beads, and findings, but don't stop there. Allow yourself enough time to leisurely stroll through every aisle. There can be lots of surprises. The drapery section may sell beads strung to use as tiebacks. The sewing section may have chain and interesting buttons. The bridal section has pearls and other beads. Look for steel stem wire in the artificial flower section. Those are just a few of the many things you may find in hobby stores. Keep looking around with a creative eye and mind.

Your local Goodwill store or thrift shop can be a treasure trove of buttons and beads, not to mention jewelry, both whole and broken. Check the dresses for fancy bead-work and buttons. Unless you happen upon a real find, such as a Chanel gown that is just your size, don't be afraid to take the beads and buttons off dresses and incorporate them into your jewelry.

Look around your own home and, if you're lucky enough to have one to visit, your grandmother's attic. Is there a chain you never wear that could be used to make

Please note: Cut chain is non-refundable.

a pair of chandelier earrings, or an ugly necklace from a distant relative that might be made into four or five pairs of awesome earrings or a couple of bracelets? Do you have a favorite stone that you'd like to use as the focal point in a bracelet or necklace?

Wire is usually found near bead-stringing materials in the shop. Photo courtesy The Bead Monkey.

Finally, see the Resources section at the end of the book for suppliers of jewelry findings and other supplies and for websites of interest to the jewelry maker.

To the jewelry maker, everything—whether found indoors or outdoors—is a potential gem!

2 Materials and Tools

In this chapter we describe some of the materials and tools you'll need to make jewelry, including wire, beads, and findings, as well as pliers, cutters, and other tools. While copper wire is great for practice and also makes pretty jewelry, we've used sterling silver in most of the projects in this book. You'll find lots of different beads available, and it's great fun to look at all the possibilities, but watch that credit-card limit! We explain findings in limited detail, but there are many more to choose from. Lastly, we list the tools you will need to make beads, wire, and findings into great jewelry!

WIRE

Wire comes in many sizes and shapes—square, round, half-round, double half-round, triangle, and twist. We use only round wire in the projects included here. Sterling silver, copper, or colored copper wire can be used for any of the projects. Brass and niobium are harder wires by their very nature, and are not used for the projects in this book. When you gain proficiency, you may want to try these wires, but they are somewhat difficult to work with.

Temper describes the hardness or softness of wire. Most wire comes in **dead soft**, **half-hard**, and **hard** tempers. Wire is softened by heating, or **annealing**; it's hardened by being hammered or, in the factory, by being drawn through holes in a metal draw plate. Wire hardens just by being worked (**work-hardened**). Most of the projects in this book can be made with either dead soft or half-hard wire. Wire temper is usually noted on the wire spool and is usually dead soft. Half-hard and hard wire are most often ordered from suppliers. Order wire by the foot, the ounce, or the pound. Depending on how much you purchase, the wire will be coiled or spooled. Be sure to immediately tag any wire you buy so that you'll be sure what you're working with later on.

The thickness of wire is described by **gauge**. The higher the gauge number, the thinner the wire. Below is a wire gauge chart that gives an idea of what the different gauges look like. In North America and Canada, wire is measured in gauges. However, in Europe it's measured in millimeters, so in the text we've included both gauge and millimeters for convenience.

WIRE GAUGE CHART

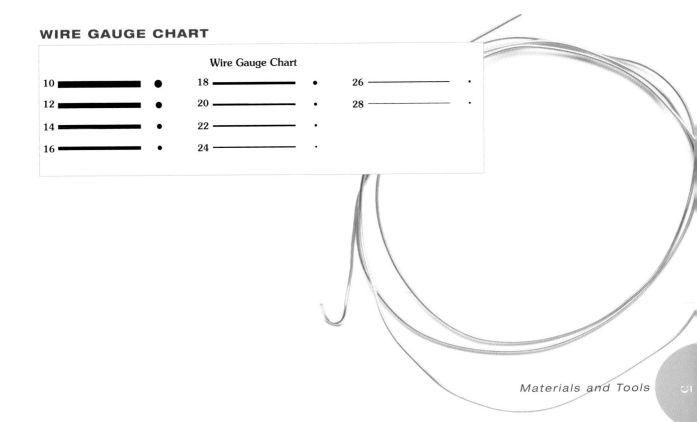

Wire Gauge Chart

10	18	26
12	20	28
14	22	
16	24	

Beads are always measured in millimeters, and they're available in almost any conceivable shape and size. Below is a chart of typical sizes and shapes. Round, square, chip, triangular, and oval are common shapes. Briolettes are pear- or teardrop-shaped beads, bicones are cone-shaped at each end, and rondelles look like bicones that have been pressed almost flat.

Beads come in different materials as well. Precious and semiprecious gems, Swarovski crystal, Austrian crystal, glass, Bali silver, bone, and metal are just a few bead materials.

MILLIMETER SIZE CHART

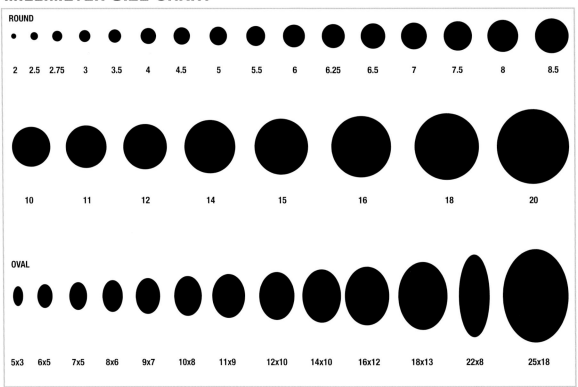

ROUND

| 2 | 2.5 | 2.75 | 3 | 3.5 | 4 | 4.5 | 5 | 5.5 | 6 | 6.25 | 6.5 | 7 | 7.5 | 8 | 8.5 |

| 10 | 11 | 12 | 14 | 15 | 16 | 18 | 20 |

OVAL

| 5x3 | 6x5 | 7x5 | 8x6 | 9x7 | 10x8 | 11x9 | 12x10 | 14x10 | 16x12 | 18x13 | 22x8 | 25x18 |

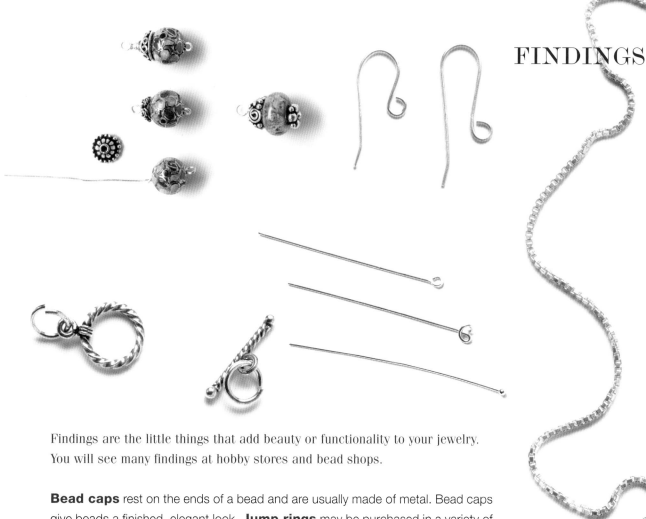

Findings are the little things that add beauty or functionality to your jewelry. You will see many findings at hobby stores and bead shops.

Bead caps rest on the ends of a bead and are usually made of metal. Bead caps give beads a finished, elegant look. **Jump rings** may be purchased in a variety of shapes and sizes. We use jump rings as connectors. **Chain** is, well, chain! We've put it under findings for convenience. In this book we use cable chain, which is chain made of simple round rings. Chains can be purchased with a clasp (finished chain) or without a clasp (bulk chain). Findings also include **ear wires, head pins, stickpins, charms,** and many more little things that you'll find helpful in making jewelry.

TOOLS

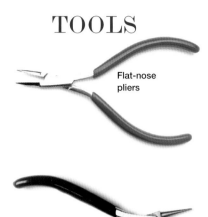

Flat-nose
pliers

Round-nose
pliers

Needle-
nose
pliers

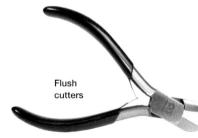

Flush
cutters

Life is always easier if you have the right tools for the job. Here are the tools we use in the projects in this book.

Flat-nose pliers are used to bend wire and hold it steady while you work on a project.

Round-nose pliers are used to create curves and loops in wire.

Needle-nose pliers are used for getting into tiny spaces, also for gripping and bending wire.

You can buy **regular wire cutters** at a hardware store and use them for making jewelry. **Flush cutters** are special wire cutters that reduce time spent filing. Their special shape means that they tend not to leave rough spots (burs) that need to be filed smooth. Whether you choose regular wire cutters or flush cutters, you will reduce the need to file off burs by placing the flat side against your cuts.

Nylon-jaw pliers are used for straightening wire. Just draw the wire through the pliers gently and slowly. They're also used with colored copper wire to prevent marring the wire.

A **jeweler's flat file** is used to smooth any rough spots that result from cutting.

An assortment of **sandpaper** helps to smooth out rough spots.

Nylon-jaw
pliers

Jeweler's flat file

Use an **Opti-Visor** or other magnifying device to better see your work and help prevent eyestrain.

Clear **safety glasses** protect your eyes from flying debris and other dangers. Wear them all the time. They will fit under an Opti-Visor. Remember: Magnifying devices are not a substitute for safety glasses!

A **rubber mallet** is used in the bangle-bracelet project to form the wire into a circle. You can also use a rubber mallet to hammer dents out of a car, which is the mallet's real purpose. Rubber mallets are available in hardware and automotive stores.

One of those fat **nail files** that have different degrees of roughness on each end are great for putting a final shine and smoothness on metal.

A **ring mandrel** is used in the knot ring project. Ring mandrels are used to shape and size rings and are marked with ring sizes. We use two different mandrels in the project, but the stepped wooden mandrel is really all you need.

A **jig** is a simple piece of plastic or wood with holes every quarter-inch in which metal pegs or nails are inserted. While we don't teach jig methods in this book, jigs can simplify your life by helping you whip up a pair of French ear wires or two identical chandelier earrings in just a few minutes. See Resources for more information on jigs.

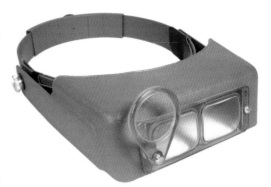
Opti-Visor

Safety glasses

Rubber mallet

Ring mandrels

3 Safety

Here are a few simple steps you can take to avoid injury while you work with sharp tools and wire.

Wear safety glasses. They are inexpensive and guard your eyes from wandering wires and flying objects.

Wear a magnifying device to prevent eyestrain. Take off the device occasionally and gaze into the distance to rest your eyes, or simply close them for a few minutes.

When you're cutting wire, **hold the wire on both sides of the cutters**. Doing so will keep those flying objects to a minimum.

Avoid an aching neck and/or back by using **good posture** while you work. Get up, walk around, and stretch every hour to relieve back tension.

Stretch your fingers as far apart as possible and then make a fist. Do so several times each hour keep your hands from cramping up. Place one hand palm down on a stable piece of furniture. Lean gently toward your fingers to stretch out your wrist. Remember to do both hands. This exercise will help you avoid carpal tunnel syndrome and prevent soreness in the wrists and forearms.

Keep small children and pets away from your work area. Neither species is famous for good judgment!

When it comes to safety, common sense is your best friend. Keep track of what you are doing and don't work with sharp objects when you are distracted or overly tired.

Be good to yourself. If you're not having fun or would rather be doing something else, stop making jewelry and come back to it later.

Safety glasses will protect
your eyes from flying objects.

4 Jump Rings

Purchasing large jump rings, like the ones we've made here, can be very expensive. It's a good idea to know how to make them.

Figure 1. Press the wire against the rod with your thumb.

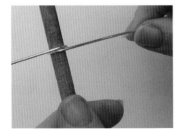

Figure 2. Begin wrapping at the center of the wire.

Materials
- 18-gauge (1.02 mm) dead soft sterling silver or copper wire

Tools
- Ruler
- Flush cutters or wire cutters
- Nylon-jaw pliers
- ⅜" (1 cm) wooden dowel
- Needle-nose pliers
- Jeweler's flat file
- Fine grit sandpaper
- Flat-nose pliers

To make six to ten jump rings, use a ruler to measure a 6" (15 cm) length of 18-gauge (1.02 mm) sterling silver wire; cut it with the wire cutters. Clean and straighten the wire with nylon-jaw pliers. With your dominant thumb, press the center of the wire against the dowel (Figure 1).

Begin wrapping the wire tightly around the dowel rod, keeping each wrap tight against the one next to it. When you have finished wrapping half the wire, turn the dowel around and repeat the process (Figure 2).

Wrapping from the center is much easier than starting at one end of the wire—working with half the wire increases your control.

Figure 3. Use needle-nose pliers to press the ends against the dowel.

Figure 4. Finished wraps.

Figure 5. Align the cutters against a wire end.

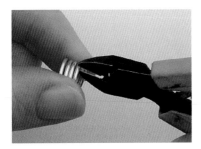

Figure 6. Cut through each wrap carefully.

When you have finished wrapping, use needle-nose pliers to press the ends of the wire against the dowel (Figure 3).

Figure 4 shows the finished wraps. They're tight, even, and close together.

Line up the cutters with the very end of the wire (Figure 5) and carefully cut through each wrap. Making the cuts as straight as possible will help reduce the amount of filing and sanding you will have to do later.

Hold the wraps as shown in Figure 6 and cut through each wrap, letting the rings fall on the work surface.

Hold a ring as shown in Figures 7 and 8, and gently move the ends **vertically** with the fingers of one hand pressing up and the fingers of the other hand pressing down. **Do not pull the ring ends apart horizontally.** The jump ring ends must be absolutely smooth so that they meet perfectly, with no space between. You will find a little rough spot, or bur, on each end from cutting.

File each end with a jeweler's flat file, using short, forward strokes (Figure 9). Do not file back and forth—always file in the same direction. Filing

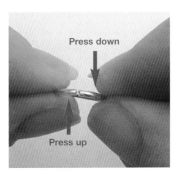

Figure 7. Hold the jump ring as shown.

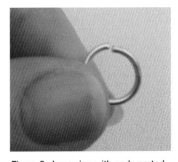

Figure 8. Jump ring with ends parted vertically.

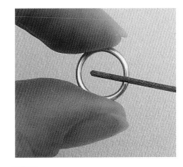

Figure 9. File the burs off the jump ring ends.

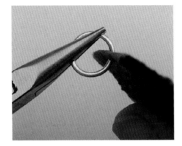

Figure 10. Use fine grit sandpaper to further smooth the ends.

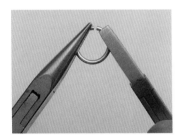

Figure 11. Jump ring ready to close.

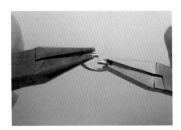

Figure 12. Move the ends up and down.

Figure 13. Press the ends toward and slightly past each other.

in different directions, using long strokes, or filing back and forth curves the ring ends. Once curved, the ends will never meet smoothly and the jump ring will not work as intended.

After filing, use fine grit sandpaper to further smooth the jump ring ends (Figure 10). Figure 11 shows a jump ring opening that is smooth, straight, and ready to close. Since this is a heavy jump ring, we're using two pairs of pliers—needle-nose on the left and flat-nose on the right. You may use any pliers except round-nose pliers, which will mar the wire. Just be sure to grasp a good portion of the jump ring for maximum control.

Use the pliers to move the jump ring ends up and down (Figures 12). At the same time push the ends slightly together, then even slightly past each other (Figure 13). You should feel a click or snap when the two ends meet properly.

Often, even after all the work you've done, the ends won't meet perfectly once they're closed (Figure 14). To fix this, use flat-nose pliers to gently adjust the higher end (Figure 15), then place the ring inside the pliers to flatten it (Figure 16).

Figure 14. These ends don't meet perfectly.

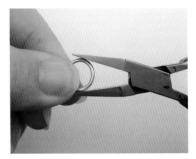

Figure 15. Gently adjust the higher end.

Figure 16. Flatten the join with pliers.

You can purchase small jump rings at hobby stores or through jewelry manufacturers. We use small, oval jump rings in several projects. They are inexpensive compared to the time you would invest in making each one.

Connecting Beads

Materials

- 20-gauge (0.812 mm) round dead soft wire—copper, colored copper, or sterling silver when you feel that you've mastered the techniques
- Round beads (we've used 7mm onyx)
- 22-gauge (0.644 mm) round dead soft or half-hard wire—same metals as above

Tools

- Ruler
- Flush or wire cutters
- Nylon-jaw pliers
- Jeweler's flat file
- Round-nose pliers
- Felt-tipped marker (such as a Sharpie)
- Needle-nose pliers

In this chapter you'll learn several ways to connect beads with wire in order to construct bracelets and necklaces. These techniques are simple, but very powerful. Use any beads you wish, and don't worry too much about diameters or sizes.

If you choose to use small beads, you'll probably want to make small loops. Large beads will require somewhat larger loops. Just be consistent and use your eyes to judge what is pleasing for you.

When you master the techniques in this chapter, you'll feel like a pro!

BASIC BEAD LOOP

Figure 1. Hold pliers correctly.

Figure 2. Insert the wire from the left.

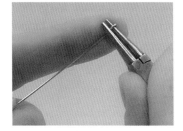

Figure 3. Rolling the wire.

Figure 4. The P-loop.

With a ruler, measure a 1½" (3.8 cm) length of 20-gauge (0.812 mm) wire and cut it with flush cutters. This amount should be more than enough for one bead component. Straighten the wire with nylon-jaw pliers and file the ends smooth with a jeweler's flat file.

You're going to make a P-loop with a ⅛" (3 mm) inside diameter. It will take a little experimentation to find the spot that gives you a ⅛" (3 mm) loop on the round-nose pliers. Start by measuring about ¼" (6 mm) from the tip; when you find the right spot, mark it with a felt-tipped marker.

It's very important to hold the pliers correctly. You should be able to see your fingertips and the palm of your hand (Figure 1).

Insert the wire into the pliers from the left and hold the pliers against your left index finger (Figure 2). Notice that only the very tip of the wire is outside the pliers.

Roll the pliers and wire toward you by slowly turning your right hand until the palm of your hand is down and you can see the back of your hand (Figure 3).

Figure 4 shows the finished P-loop. The loop should measure about ⅛" (3 mm) inside diameter.

Figure 5. Closing the P-loop.

Figure 6. Close the loop completely.

Figure 7. Grasp P-loop with needle-nose pliers.

Figure 8. Still bending, but almost through.

By itself, the P-loop is useless, but almost all loops start with the P-loop.

Notice the finger holding the wire tightly against the pliers. This position affords the best control. Roll the pliers until you can't roll anymore. Reposition the pliers as necessary and continue to roll the wire until the loop is closed (Figure 5).

You may need to squeeze the loop with the needle-nose pliers to finish closing the gap. Squeeze gently so you don't squash the loop (Figure 6)!

To center the loop, support the wire with your left index finger and bend the loop to one side (Figures 7 and 8) until it is centered on the wire (Figure 9). Always use needle-nose pliers for bending—round-nose pliers can mar the wire.

We're using 7mm onyx beads, but you can use any bead that's round. Put a bead on the wire and move it as close as possible to the loop.

We have a little problem here: The bead won't snug up tightly against the loop. This means there's a curve at the base of the loop (Figure 10). We need to give the loop a sharper, more defined beginning.

Use needle-nose pliers to flatten the wire at the base of the loop (Figure 11). You may have to reclose the loop after you've made this correction.

Figure 12 shows the finished loop with the bead in the proper position.

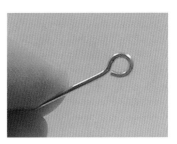

Figure 9. The centered loop.

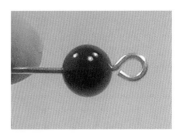

Figure 10. Problem: bead does not fit snugly against the loop.

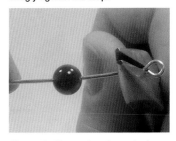

Figure 11. Flatten the wire at the base of the loop.

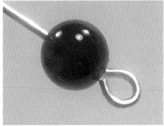

Figure 12. Finished loop with bead snugged up tightly.

Connecting Beads

Figure 13. Place the needle-nose pliers close to the bead.

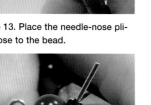
Figure 14. Start bending the second loop.

Figure 15. Find the marked spot on the pliers.

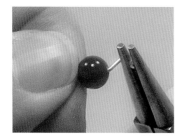
Figure 16. Begin rolling the wire down toward the bead.

To make the loop on the other end of the bead, we're going to do everything we've done so far, but in reverse. Use the needle-nose pliers to bend the wire in the opposite direction from the first loop (Figures 13 and 14). Make sure that the loops are exactly opposite and lined up with each other.

Caution: Be careful not to exert too much pressure on the bead while you're bending the wire—you run the risk of breaking the bead.

Find the spot you marked earlier on the round-nose pliers and place the very tip of the wire at that spot (Figure 15). Begin rolling the wire down toward the bead (Figure 16). Reposition the pliers as needed to complete the loop (Figure 17). Making the loops the same shape and size may take a little practice.

Now do a little adjusting where necessary. Flatten the loops by squeezing gently with needle-nose pliers (Figure 18). Use the pliers to align the loops evenly along the same plane. If necessary, use round-nose pliers to realign and round the loops. Figure 19 shows the finished bead with loops.

Figure 17. Reposition the pliers as necessary.

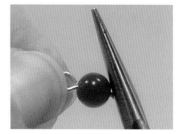
Figure 18. Flatten the loops.

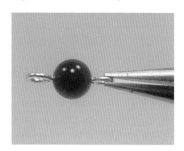
Figure 19. The finished bead with loops.

Getting Started Making Wire Jewelry

You may not want to hear this, but if the loops don't look right to you, just cut off the wire and start over. Each time you start over, you'll learn something new, and it will get easier—really!

Figure 20. Open one loop.

When you have finished several beads with loops, you can join them together. Use needle-nose pliers to open a loop in the manner described for opening jump rings on page 14 (Figure 20). For good control be sure to grasp about half the wire loop with the pliers.

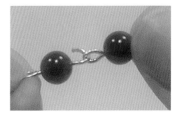

Figure 21. Slip the open loop through a closed loop.

Slip the open loop through a closed loop and reclose the open loop as you learned to do with jump rings (Figures 21 and 22).

Figure 22. Reclose the open loop.

With the needle-nose pliers, close the loop completely (Figure 23).

You can continue to join beads with loops to make a bracelet or necklace. Now, let's add another technique to make things a little more interesting.

Figure 23. Close the loop completely.

MAKING AN S-HOOK

Figure 24. Make a P-loop and cut a ⅜" (1 cm) length.

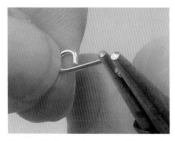

Figure 25. Round-nose pliers about to start the loop.

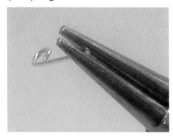

Figure 26. Curve the second P-loop in the opposite direction.

Make a P-loop just as before—use the same mark on the round-nose pliers to position the wire. Measure ⅜" (1 cm) from the loop, cut with flush cutters, and file the end smooth with the jeweler's flat file (Figure 24).

Form another P-loop curving in the opposite direction at the other end of the wire (Figures 25 and 26).

Figure 27 shows the S-hook almost finished. Use needle-nose pliers to further close the loop. If necessary, use round-nose pliers to round out the loops.

Be sure that the S-hook is flat. If it isn't, press it with needle-nose pliers (Figure 28).

Open one end of the S-hook and slip the open end into a bead loop (Figure 29). Close the S-hook the way you closed the jump ring (see page 14).

Figure 30 shows two different strands of beads. You can see how adding the S-hooks to a strand creates a totally different look.

With the techniques you've learned so far, you have the knowledge to make several styles of bracelets or necklaces. Now you'll learn another technique that will add even more variety to your jewelry.

Figure 27. Closing the second loop.

Figure 28. Flatten the connector.

Figure 29. Add an S-hook to a bead with loops.

Figure 30. Blue strand with S-hooks, black strand with plain loops.

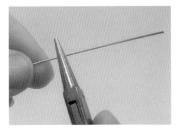

Figure 31. Grasp the wire at the 1½" (3.8 cm) mark.

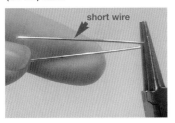

Figure 32. Short wire on top.

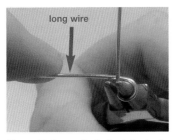

Figure 33. Long wire to the left; short wire straight up.

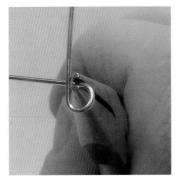

Figure 34. Place needle-nose pliers on the loop.

Use 22-gauge (0.644 mm) dead soft or half-hard wire. Experience will teach you the temper you prefer. You can use the same beads here that you used for the beads with loops.

Cut a piece of wire about 12" (30.5 cm) long. Mark the wire 1½" (3.8 cm) from the end. Mark the round-nose pliers about ¼" (6 mm) from the tip of the jaws.

Place the wire in the pliers and line up the mark on the wire with the mark on the pliers (Figure 31). Start making a loop by bending the short wire around the pliers, then up. The long wire piece should be pointing to the left, and the short wire should cross in front of the long wire (Figure 32).

Keep rotating your hand until the short end of the wire is facing straight up and the long end is on the left side (Figure 33).

Use needle-nose pliers to grip the loop as in Figure 34. Bend the loop up slightly to create an angle on the long-wire side of the loop (Figure 35). Doing so will give the loop a nice rounded appearance. Now place the needle-nose pliers across half the loop to support it while you begin to wrap (Figure 36).

Begin wrapping by bringing the short wire to the back of the long wire and then down (Figure 37).

WRAPPED BEAD LOOP

Figure 35. Bend the loop to create an angle.

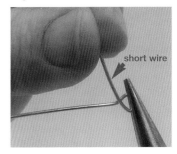

Figure 36. Place pliers across half the loop.

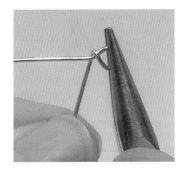

Figure 37. Bring the short wire behind and down.

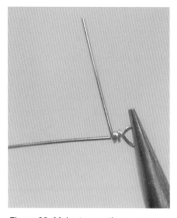

Figure 38. Make two or three wraps.

Figure 39. Cut off excess wire.

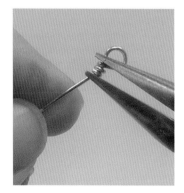

Figure 40. Press the wraps together if necessary.

Bring the short wire up and keep wrapping until you have two or three wraps (Figure 38). Wrap tightly against the long wire and keep the wraps as close together as possible.

After you've finished wrapping, cut off the rest of the short wire. Remember that the flat side of the cutters should face the work (Figure 39). Press the cut wire down in place with needle-nose pliers.

If necessary, keep using the needle-nose pliers to squeeze the wraps together toward the loop (Figure 40). Use round-nose pliers to re-round the loop if needed.

Slide a bead onto the wire and up against the wraps (Figure 41).

Now use the needle-nose pliers to start another loop (Figure 42). Remember to start the loop on the marked spot on the pliers. Start this loop far enough back on the wire to leave room for the wraps, about ⅛" to ¼" (3 to 6 mm).

This process may take a little practice. We want the same number of wraps on each side of the bead, hopefully with no extra space between the wraps and the bead.

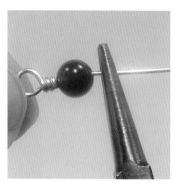

Figure 41. Slide a bead onto the wire against the wraps.

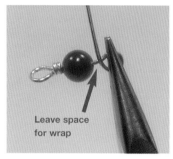

Leave space for wrap

Figure 42. Beginning the wrap on the other side of the bead.

Figure 43. Wrapping the other end.

Wrap the other end of the bead exactly the same as you wrapped the first end (Figure 43).

Figure 44 shows the finished bead.

You can link these beads by slipping the wire of one bead through the loop in another (Figure 45) before wrapping, then simply make a loop and wraps as before. It may feel a little awkward at first, but the process of connecting beads will become very easy, very quickly.

If you forget to connect one bead to another (and you will), no problem! Just connect to either wrapped end the next time.

Figure 46 shows two connected beads.

Figure 44. The finished bead.

Figure 45. Linking beads and wrapping them.

Figure 46. Two connected beads.

Connecting Beads

6

Head Pins

Head pins are wires with a "head" on one end that holds beads in place. The head can be simple or ornate. Head pins are very handy findings to have around. You can use them as dangles on earrings and to attach embellishments for bracelets and necklaces.

Materials

• About 3" (7.5 cm) 16-gauge (1.29 mm) dead soft sterling silver wire

• Bali beads (Bali silver beads are traditionally made in Indonesia and are available at most bead shops and hobby stores. Here we are using "quads," four little beads soldered together to make a square.)

Tools

• Ruler

• Flush or wire cutters

• Needle-nose pliers

• Round-nose pliers

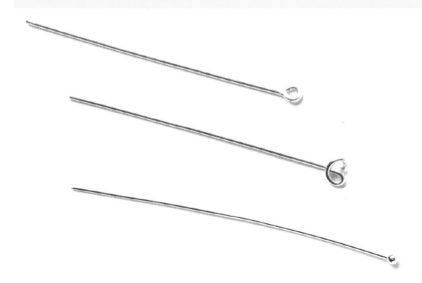

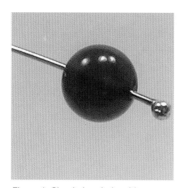

Figure 1. Simple head pin with ball end.

Figure 2. Head pin as finished bead bangle.

Figure 3. Same head pin with Bali bead added.

Figure 1 shows a bead on a plain head pin with a simple ball end, and Figure 2 shows the beaded head pin finished with a wrapped loop.

You can make this simple head pin look more interesting by adding Bali beads (Figure 3). This particular head pin was store-bought, but buying head pins can get expensive. It's nice to know how to make your own.

You can make a very simple head pin like the one in Figure 4. Use the smallest end on either needle- or round-nose pliers. Measure and cut a 3" (7.5-cm) piece of 16-gauge (1.29 mm) dead soft wire.

Place the end into the very end of the pliers (Figure 5).

Make a P-loop (see page 16 for instructions) and bend the loop back a little to center it (Figure 6). Usually a 3" (7.5 cm) piece of wire will be plenty to make any head pin, but by making them yourself, you can cut the wire to whatever length you need.

From the techniques you've learned in previous chapters, you can see how you can keep adding beads to the loop, or perhaps charms—use your imagination and you'll come up with plenty of other ideas.

Figure 4. Simple head pin with loop end.

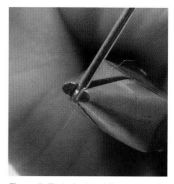

Figure 5. End of wire at the very end of pliers.

Figure 6. Make a P-loop.

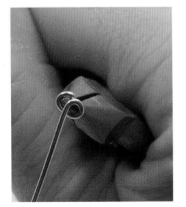

Figure 7. Curl the wire all the way around the pliers.

Here's a head pin with a double loop end.

Again, use the very smallest end of either round- or needle-nose pliers and place the very end of the wire inside the tip of the pliers.

Hold the wire tightly and curl the wire all the way around the end of the pliers (Figure 7).

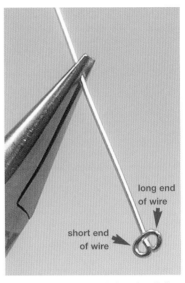

long end of wire

short end of wire

Figure 9. Finished double-loop head pin.

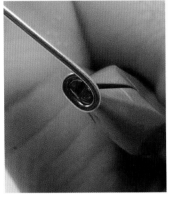

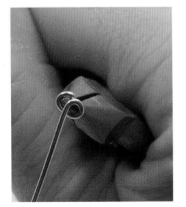

Figure 8. Use the pliers to center the loops and bring the long part of the head pin through the middle of the pliers.

Use pliers to press, pull, and push the loops until they are centered, then bring the long part of the head pin through the middle of the pliers (Figure 8).

Gently flatten the loops against the wire and make any adjustments necessary so the two loops are symmetrical. Figure 9 shows the finished double-loop head pin and Figure 10 shows how the head pin looks with a bead.

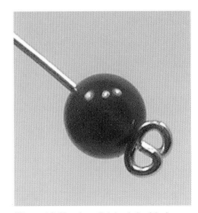

Figure 10. Bead on finished double-loop head pin.

Four finished head pins on French ear wires.

Fancy beads on ball-end head pins with Bali bead caps.

7

Coils

A finished coil.

This coil is commonly used as an embellishment, but you can also use it to make earrings or incorporate it into other jewelry. Coils can be used as bead caps, and they look great when hammered. Making coils is a great way to practice jewelry-making skills. Coils also come in handy for finishing off wire ends. One caveat—coils can snag and come uncoiled. To prevent snagging, hammer the coil to work-harden it. Coating the back of the coil with clear two-part epoxy will also help the coil to keep its shape.

Materials
- 20-gauge (0.812 mm) or larger dead soft wire

Tools
- Wire cutters
- Needle-nose pliers
- Flat-nose pliers
- Rubber mallet and/or regular hammer (if desired)
- Jeweler's flat file

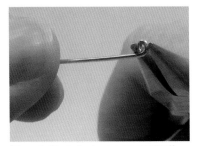

Cut a length of 20-gauge (0.812 mm) dead soft wire appropriate to the size coil you want to make. You can cut the wire blunt or, to make a perfectly solid loop, cut the wire at an angle. Make a tiny loop around the end of round- or needle-nose pliers. If desired, use needle-nose pliers to make the loop even smaller (Figure 1).

Figure 1. Pinch the loop even smaller if desired.

Grasp the loop with needle-nose pliers, leaving just a little of the loop exposed. Use your thumb or index finger to press the wire against the loop, beginning the coil (Figure 2).

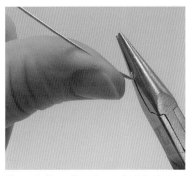

Figure 2. Press the wire against the loop.

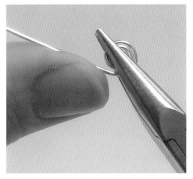

Figure 3. Continue to press the wire against the coil.

Figure 4. You may want to switch to flat-nose pliers for better control.

Continue to press the wire against the coil, adjusting the pliers as necessary (Figure 3). The more of the coil that's inside the pliers, the less likely the coil is to slip. At this point you may want to switch to flat-nose pliers for better control (Figure 4).

If you see a gap where the wire isn't touching the preceding winding (Figure 5), simply grasp the wire and pull it to the front of the spiral and then to the back. Replace the wire against the spiral and you should have a closer fit (Figures 6 through 8). Just remember to watch for this gap problem and fix it immediately—it won't be possible to go back and fix it later.

If a coil doesn't seem strong enough to hold its shape, you probably need to use a heavier-gauge wire. Another alternative is to work-harden the coil by placing it between two sheets of metal and tapping it with a rubber mallet. You can get interesting effects by placing the coil on a hard metal surface and using a regular hammer. Hammering may cause unwanted marring of the metal, but on the other hand, marring sometimes gives the metal an attractive effect. File any rough spots with a jeweler's flat file.

There is no set size for a coil. Depending on its intended use, you can make it as large or small as you wish.

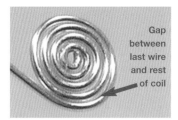

Figure 5. The last wire needs to be closer to the rest of the coil.

Figure 6. Fixing a gap in the coil. Bring the wire forward.

Figure 7. Bring the wire to the back.

Figure 8. Place the wire back against the coil.

8

French Ear Wires

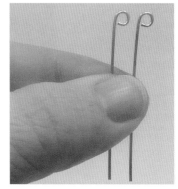

These wires are the foundation for most of the earrings you will make. They can be purchased at hobby stores and bead shops, but we provide instructions in case you prefer to make your own or have a project that requires a custom ear wire. French ear wires are shaped in such a way that they do not need a closing mechanism— they simply slide through the ear and stay in place.

Always use sterling silver, stainless steel, gold, or gold-filled wire for ear wires to lessen the chance of infection or other reactions to the metal.

Materials

- Two 2" lengths of 20-gauge (0.812 mm) wire (preferably half-hard, but dead soft will do).

Tools

- Ruler
- Flush or wire cutters
- Plastic darning needle (or ⅛" [3 mm] diameter wooden dowel)
- ⅜" (1 cm) diameter wooden dowel
- Flat-nose pliers
- Jeweler's flat file
- Isopropyl alcohol

To make ear wires that match, you must make both at the same time. With the ruler, measure two 2" (5 cm) pieces of 20-gauge (0.812 mm) wire and cut them with the flush or wire cutters. Make a ⅛" (3 mm) P-loop on one end of each wire (Figure 1) following the instructions on page 16.

Figure 1. Make P-loops on the end of both wires.

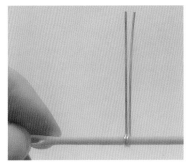

Figure 2. Use a ⅛" (3 mm) plastic darning needle to roll the P-loops into snug, round circles.

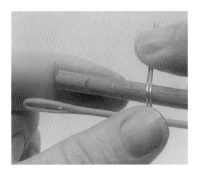

Figure 3. Wooden dowel rod and darning needle with wire. Begin to wrap the wires over the dowel.

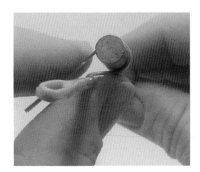

Figure 4. Curve until the wires almost meet the loops.

Insert a darning needle (or ⅛" [3 mm] diameter dowel) through the P-loops and roll the wire snugly around the needle until you have nicely defined circles (Figure 2).

Hold the ⅜" (1 cm) wooden dowel parallel to the darning needle. Leave a ¼" (6 mm) to ½" (1.3 cm) space between the dowel and the darning needle. Hold the darning needle and dowel with your left hand and begin to curve the wires over the dowel with your right hand (Figure 3).

Keep curving the wires around the dowel until the wires almost meet the loops on the back (Figure 4).

Figure 5 shows the front of the work.

Figure 6 shows the ear wires with the dowel removed. They look fairly identical.

In Figure 7, you can see that the ear wire on the left is slightly off-center.

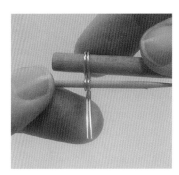

Figure 5. The front of the work.

Figure 6. Both ear wires with the dowel removed.

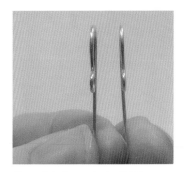

Figure 7. Left ear wire is slightly off-center.

Figure 8. Flatten any crooked areas with flat-nose pliers.

Figure 9. Both ear wires together.

Figure 10. Measure $\frac{13}{16}$" (2.1 cm) from the top; cut.

To fix the problem, just press the offending ear wire between the jaws of the flat-nose pliers (Figure 8).

Figure 9 shows the ear wires placed together. They are virtually identical.

With a ruler, measure $\frac{13}{16}$" (2.1 cm) from the top of each ear wire and cut off any excess wire (Figure 10). File and smooth the ends of both ear wires with the jeweler's flat file.

Use flat-nose pliers to make a slight curve at the end of each ear wire. If you line up the pliers with the very end of an ear wire as in Figure 11, your ear wires will have the same curve every time. Clean the wires with alcohol.

Figure 12 shows the pliers with the curve completed, and Figure 13 shows the finished ear wires.

This project takes just a little practice, especially in holding the dowel and darning needle at the same time. Once you've mastered that, you'll be making ear wires quickly and easily.

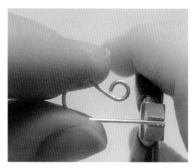

Figure 11. Align the end of the wire with the far side of the pliers.

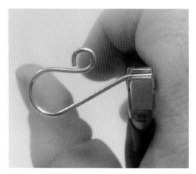

Figure 12. Make a slight curve at the end of the ear wire.

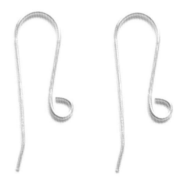

Figure 13. The finished ear wires.

Some earrings made with French ear wires.

Round Ear Wires

Sometimes French ear wires just aren't right for an earring design. Round ear wires broaden design possibilities and give earrings a totally different look. These round ear wires are ½" (1.3 cm) in diameter, but they can be made as large or small as you wish by using larger or smaller dowels for wrapping.

Always use sterling silver, stainless steel, gold, or gold-filled wire for ear wires to lessen the chance of infection or other reactions to the metal.

Materials

- 20-gauge (0.812 mm) dead soft wire

Tools

- Ruler
- Flush or wire cutters
- ½" (1.3 cm) dowel
- Jeweler's flat file
- Round-nose pliers
- Felt-tipped marker (such as a Sharpie)
- Needle-nose pliers
- Fingernail file
- Isopropyl alcohol

With the ruler, measure 6" (15 cm) of 20-gauge (0.812 mm) dead soft wire, cut it with the wire cutters, and wrap it around a ½" (1.3 cm) dowel three times using medium tension. After wrapping, let the wire spring back into a looser tension on the dowel rod (Figure 1).

Figure 1. Wrap the wire around the dowel rod three times.

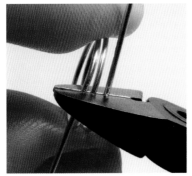

Figure 2. Hold the loops and cut through them.

Figure 3. Starting a P-loop.

Figure 4. The P-loop finished.

Figure 5. Centering the P-loop.

Remove the wire loops from the dowel rod and hold them together snugly while cutting through them (Figure 2). File the ends smooth with the jeweler's flat file.

Find a spot on the round-nose pliers about ¼" (6 mm) from the tips that will make a loop about ⅜" (1 cm) in diameter; mark the pliers with a felt-tipped marker. Place the wire inside the pliers at this mark and make a P-loop (Figures 3 and 4).

Center the loop with needle-nose pliers (Figure 5). Round and reclose the loop if necessary (Figure 6).

The end that goes through the ear must be very smooth. After filing the end flat, use a fingernail file to smooth any rough spots (Figure 7).

Use needle-nose pliers to turn up the end just enough to fit securely in the loop, but not so much that the wire will not go through the ear easily (Figures 8 and 9).

Clean the wire with alcohol and practice putting it on. Press the wire more open or more closed, gradually and gently with your fingers, until the end of the earring wire goes easily through your ear and fits securely in the loop.

Figure 6. Reclosing the P-loop.

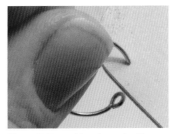

Figure 7. Smoothing the end with a fingernail file.

Figure 8. Bend up the very end of the earring.

Figure 9. Bend up the very end of the earring.

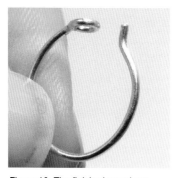

Figure 10 shows the finished round ear wire.

Figure 11 shows an embellished bead hanging from the ear wire.

Figure 10. The finished round ear wire.

Figure 11. Embellished bead on a round ear wire.

Earrings using round ear wires.

Large Bead-Hole Problems

Figure 1. Problem bead.

10

Materials
- Problem bead with large hole
- 22-gauge (0.644 mm) dead soft wire
- Bead cap
- Small beads

Tools
- Ruler
- Felt-tipped marker (such as a Sharpie)
- Flush or wire cutters
- Round-nose pliers
- Flat-nose pliers
- Needle-nose pliers

Into every jewelry maker's life a little problem or two will fall. In this case, we've found a beautiful bead that we would love to use in a project. The bead hole, however, is the size of the chunnel between England and France! Are we exaggerating? Yes! Are we worried? Of course not! Here's an answer to the problem of overly large bead holes.

Here's our problem bead. As Figure 1 shows, the wire is much too thin for the huge hole. The bead will wobble unless we make the wire fill the hole.

Use the ruler to measure the bead. With the wire cutters, cut a piece of 22-gauge (0.644 mm) dead soft wire three times the length of the bead.

Multiply the length of the bead by two and mark this length on the wire with a felt-tipped marker. Then mark the midpoint between this mark and the shorter end of the wire. The midpoint should be about equal to the length of the bead. Make a small loop at the midpoint with round-nose pliers (Figure 2).

Figure 2. Make a small loop in the middle of the wire.

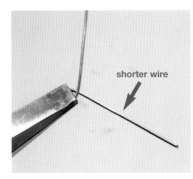

Figure 3. Hold the loop firmly with flat-nose pliers.

Figure 4. Twist the wires.

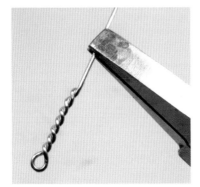

Figure 5. The loop and twisted wire.

Hold the loop firmly with flat-nose pliers as in Figure 3.

Twist the wires. The twist should be straight and even. Try to maintain a 90° angle where the wires cross (Figure 4).

When the twist is as long as the bead hole, cut off the shorter wire with the wire cutters. Use flat-nose pliers to straighten both the twisted wires and the single longer wire (Figure 5).

Thread the twisted wire into the bead hole. In Figure 6, you can see the twisted wire just slightly. You can embellish with a wrapped loop here, just as you learned to do in the Connecting Beads section (see pages 21 to 23).

Figure 7 shows a bead cap added to the bead. The hole in the bead cap is also too large for the wire. To solve this problem, add a small bead that fits snugly into the hole or rests on top of the bead-cap hole.

After adding the small bead, you can make a wrapped loop to finish the bead (Figure 8).

Use round-nose pliers to center the loops and round them.

Figure 6. The twisted wire inside the bead hole.

Figure 7. Bead cap and bead added.

Figure 8. The finished bead with bead cap.

Wrapping Briolettes

11

Briolettes are teardrop-shaped gemstones with a hole drilled through the narrow end at the top. While lovely, they require a special technique to be turned into useful components for jewelry. The unique shape of the briolette presents several problems when you're wrapping, but using briolettes is worth the hassle for their graceful shape. We'll show how to wrap a briolette and then discuss the problems afterward.

Materials

- 22-gauge (0.812 mm) dead soft wire
- Briolettes of your choice

Tools

- Ruler
- Flush or wire cutters
- Round-nose pliers
- Needle-nose pliers

For this project, we've used a large man-made stone with a hole that will accommodate 22-gauge (0.644 mm) wire. Measure with the ruler a piece of wire about 5" (12.5 cm) long. Cut the wire at an angle with the flush cutters. Run the wire through the hole as in Figure 1, leaving at least ½" (1.3 cm) or more on the left side.

Using your fingers, bend the left side up, then bend the right side up and in front of the left wire (Figures 2 and 3). The wires should cross each other more than 90°.

Figure 1. Insert the wire through the hole.

Figure 2. Bend up the left side.

Figure 3. Bring up the right side in front of the left side.

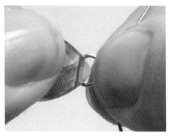

Figure 4. Twist both wires clockwise.

Figure 5. Making the second twist.

With your fingers, grasp the wires where they cross and twist both wires clockwise. Make two complete twists (Figures 4 through 6).

Figure 7 shows how the front of the stone should look at this point.

Cut off the short wire very close to the twist (Figure 8) with the flush cutters.

Use round-nose pliers to straighten the remaining wire (Figure 9).

Figure 6. Two twists completed.

Figure 7. Front of the stone.

Figure 8. Cut off the short wire.

Figure 9. Straighten the remaining wire.

Figure 10. Position pliers to start a loop.

Figure 11. Completing a loop.

Figure 12. Bringing the wire across.

Figure 13. A view of the back.

Position the pliers to start a loop and bend the wire to the side (Figure 10).

Form a loop by using the round-nose pliers, as shown earlier in the Wrapped Bead Loop section of Chapter 5, Connecting Beads on pages 21 to 23 (Figure 11).

Place needle-nose pliers across the loop to hold it in place while you bring the wire across (Figure 12).

Figure 13 shows the back of the loop. Round and center the loop with round-nose pliers (Figure 14).

Start wrapping over the twisted wire (Figures 15 and 16) as you did in the Wrapped Bead Loop section of Chapter 5, Connecting Beads (see pages 21 to 23).

If the wraps become uneven, use needle-nose pliers to press them into place (Figures 17 and 18). Keep wrapping over the twisted wire toward the stone.

Figure 14. Round and center the loop.

Figure 15. Starting the wrap.

Figure 16. First wrap finished.

Figure 17. Uneven wrap being pressed back into place.

Figure 18. Wrap back in place.

Figure 19. Closing a space in the wrap.

Figure 20. Completed wraps. Cut on the back side.

Figure 21. Press end firmly into place.

Figure 19 shows the back of the stone with a space in the wrap that needs to be closed. Use needle-nose pliers to close the space.

Figure 20 shows the wraps completed. Cut the wire on the back of the stone, never on the side or the front.

Use needle-nose pliers to press the wire end firmly in place (Figure 21).

Figure 22 shows the finished wraps on the back.

Figure 23 shows the front of the wrap. The wraps look great, but the wires coming out of the briolette are off-center. To compensate, move the top loop slightly to the right so that the stone will be centered when it's hung from an ear wire or bracelet. Even with practice, off-centered wires will still happen occasionally.

If it's any comfort, the off-centered wires will not really be noticeable to anyone but you. We're using a very large stone with a very heavy gauge wire, and we're taking pictures that are many times enlarged. Feel better?

Figure 24 shows the wrapped briolette on an ear wire.

Figure 22. The finished wraps on the back side.

Figure 23. Front view.

Figure 24. The finished briolette on an ear wire.

Getting Started Making Wire Jewelry

The Awful Truth
about Stones

This project is not easy. More accurately, the project is easy, but the briolettes are difficult to work with. Because the hole is drilled at the weakest spot on the stone, briolettes break very easily.

The holes drilled in natural gemstones are not usually consistent. If the hole is drilled straight across, one end will most likely be narrower than the other. Sometimes the holes are drilled first from the left side and then from the right side; holes drilled this way don't always meet in the middle.

When you're working with a natural gemstone, it is wise to use a small-gauge wire such as 24- or 26-gauge. Cut the wire end at an angle and use a nail file to narrow the end. Hopefully, the wire will go through the hole easily. Never try to force the wire—you'll likely break the stone.

The moral of the story is: Be prepared for problems when you're using natural gemstones. If you want to avoid problems, use man-made stones such as Swarovski crystals. They are very precisely made by an accurate machine process and are quite beautiful.

Why go through all this? Because the briolette is one of the most beautiful and effective shapes to use in jewelry. Just be very careful when you're choosing stones. If you're lucky enough to live near a bead shop, take a piece of wire with you and check the holes yourself!

12

Swirl Bead

Swirl bead on a round ear wire.

This is a simple but elegant embellishment that turns an ordinary bead into something special. The swirl will work on any smooth bead. (Faceted beads look rather odd done this way, so we don't recommend adding swirls to them.) Use the swirl bead on earrings, bracelets, and necklaces and turn something plain into something extraordinary!

Materials

- 6mm or 7mm bead of your choice
- 3" or 4" (7.5 cm or 10 cm) head pin of your choice, purchased or handmade, of a gauge that will fit inside the bead you've chosen

Tools

- Needle-nose pliers
- Flush or wire cutters

Thread the bead onto the head pin (Figure 1). Use needle-nose pliers to make a plain loop (Figure 2). Use pliers marked as described for Connecting Beads earlier in the book (see page 16).

Hold the loop with needle-nose pliers and hold the end of the wire with your fingers. Doing so will give the swirl a natural gracefulness (Figure 3).

Bring the wire around the loop to make a complete swirl at the bottom of the loop (Figure 4). Try to make this top swirl graceful, but not tight.

Figure 1. Thread the bead onto the head pin.

Figure 2. Make a plain loop.

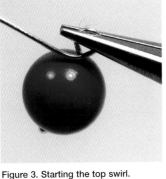

Figure 3. Starting the top swirl.

Figure 4. Bring the wire around the loop.

Figure 5. Keep bringing the wire around the loop.

Keep bringing the wire around the loop, turning the bead as necessary (Figure 5).
Figure 6 shows the completed top swirl.

Still holding the loop in the pliers, use an even, strong pull to bring the wire down and around the bead (Figure 7).

Remember to swirl! We're holding the bead with pliers so you can clearly see what's happening, but holding the bead with your fingers will give you better control.

Loop the wire around the head pin end (Figure 8).

Figure 6. The top swirl is complete.

Figure 7. Pull the wire down and around the bead.

Figure 8. Loop the wire around the head pin.

Figure 9. Bringing the wire around the end of the head pin.

Figure 10. Pull the wire end across the loop.

Figure 11. Cut wire end.

Holding the bead with your fingers, use needle-nose pliers to bring the end of the wire around the head pin end until the wire crosses over the loop (Figures 9 and 10).

Keeping the flat end of the cutters toward the work, cut the end off as close as possible. Be careful not to nick or cut the remaining wire (Figure 11).

Use needle-nose pliers to press the wire end around the head pin (Figure 12).

Try hanging the bead on a French ear wire to make sure the swirl faces toward the front and not the back or the side. Adjust the top loop if necessary so the swirl faces forward. Figure 13 shows the finished bead on a French ear wire.

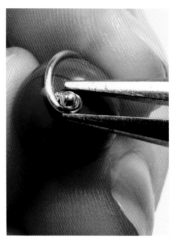

Figure 12. Press around head pin.

Figure 13. The finished swirl bead on a French ear wire.

Getting Started Making Wire Jewelry

13

Simple Clasps

Materials

- 1½" length of 16-gauge (1.29 mm) dead soft silver wire
- 16-gauge ¼" (6 mm) diameter jump ring

Tools

- Ruler
- Flush or wire cutters
- Round-nose pliers
- Felt-tipped marker (such as a Sharpie)
- Jeweler's flat file
- Needle-nose pliers

The first clasp is very easy to make. You'll probably use it often because it's very secure and easy to open and close. The second clasp is a little more difficult to make, but also fairly simple. Both clasps use the same wire gauge and jump rings.

With a ruler, measure a 1½" (3.8 cm) piece of 16-gauge (1.29 mm) wire, then cut it with the flush cutters. Make a P-loop at one end (Figure 1) with the round-nose pliers. Refer to the section Connecting Beads for instructions on making a P-loop (page 16).

Measure from the end of the P-loop to the end of the wire and mark the halfway point with a felt-tipped marker. Use the center of the round-nose pliers to form a U shape as in Figures 2 and 3.

A SIMPLE CLASP

Figure 1. Make a P-loop.

Figure 2. Make a U shape.

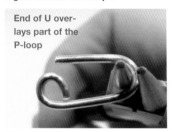

End of U over-
lays part of the
P-loop

Figure 3. Finish the U shape.

Figure 4. Use round-nose pliers to make a slight curve at the end of the wire.

Figure 5. Move the end of the wire from side to side.

The end of the U should overlay at least part of the P-loop as in Figure 3. Don't close the P-loop completely until you've attached one end of the piece to it!

With the jeweler's flat file, file the end smooth and use round-nose pliers to make a slight curve at the end of the wire (Figure 4).

Use needle-nose pliers to move the end wire from side to side and down to make a close, tight fit. This is the same method we used for closing jump rings (see page 14, Figures 12 and 13).

With the needle-nose pliers, attach the P-loop to one end of the piece and attach a jump ring to the other end.

When you insert the jump ring through the clasp, there should be some resistance before the jump ring snaps into place (Figure 7).

Figure 8 shows the finished clasp.

Figure 6. Press the wire down for a tight fit.

Figure 7. Insert a jump ring through the clasp.

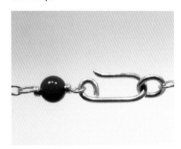

Figure 8. The finished clasp.

A NOT-AS-SIMPLE CLASP

The only tricky thing about making this clasp is finding the right support while you make the curves. Without the proper support, the piece will be uneven. Practice will make this clasp a favorite.

Measure with a ruler and then cut a 2½" (6.5 cm) piece of 16-gauge (1.29 mm) wire with the flush cutters. Find the center and make a U with round-nose pliers. The U should be made about in the middle of the pliers (Figure 9).

Cut the ends even and file them smooth with the jeweler's flat file (Figure 10).

Use the round-nose pliers to make a P-loop in each end about ⅛" (3 mm) in diameter (Figure 11).

The P-loops should be even and the same size (Figure 12).

Measure from the ends of the P-loops to the end of the U and mark the midpoint. With flat-nose pliers, hold the clasp with the jaws against the P-loops (Figure 13).

Figure 9. Make a U.

Figure 10. Even up the ends of the U-shaped wire and file them smooth.

Figure 11. Make a P-loop in each end.

Figure 12. The loops should be even and the same size.

Figure 13. Hold the clasp with flat-nose pliers.

Figure 14. Roll the wires toward the P-loops.

Figure 15. Roll the other side of the clasp.

Figure 16. Add a jump ring to the P-loops and the last link of the piece.

Place round-nose pliers at the midpoint and roll the wires toward the P-loops as shown in Figure 14.

Since the round-nose pliers are tapered, you must roll from both sides of the clasp to keep the sides even (Figure 15). Because you are working with two wires, thus a wider width, you have to bend the clasp from both sides. Reverse the clasp in the flat-nose pliers and roll a little more with the round-nose pliers. Add a jump ring to the P-loops and to the last link in the piece (Figure 16).

Use the needle-nose pliers to add another jump ring to the other end. The clasp should be tight enough that the jump ring snaps into place (Figure 17).

Figure 18 shows the finished clasp.

Figure 17. Jump ring should stop and then snap into place.

Figure 18. The finished clasp.

Getting Started Making Wire Jewelry

Toggle Clasps

14

Materials

- 18-gauge (1.02 mm) dead soft wire
- 2 purchased 18-gauge (4.1 x 2.9 mm) oval jump rings (you could make your own, but it's a lot easier to purchase this size)
- 1 purchased ¾" (2 cm) outside diameter twisted jump ring for toggle circle

Tools

- Ruler
- Flush or wire cutters
- Jeweler's flat file
- Felt-tipped marker (such as a Sharpie)
- Round-nose pliers
- Needle-nose pliers

The twisted-wire toggle adds elegance to a bracelet or necklace. Made properly, the toggle clasp is easy to open and close and holds a piece together securely. It's also very easy to make!

To make the toggle bar, measure with the ruler then cut with the flush cutters a piece of wire 1½" (3.8 cm) long. Smooth the ends with the jeweler's flat file. With a felt-tipped marker, mark the midpoint on the wire, which should be about ¾" (2 cm). Place round-nose pliers on the mark about ⅛" (6 mm) from the end of the pliers (Figure 1).

Figure 1. Place round-nose pliers at the midpoint of the wire.

Figure 2. Form a loop.

Figure 3. Press the wires slightly below the loop.

Figure 4. Use round-nose pliers to form loops at each end of the wire.

Figure 5. The finished toggle bar.

Bring the left side of the wire up and to the right. Bring the right side of the wire up and to the left. Doing so should make a loop exactly in the middle of the wire (Figure 2).

Press the wires down slightly below the loop before you remove the pliers (Figure 3).

Remove the wire from the pliers. Use the very tip of the round-nose pliers to roll the ends toward the center of the wire. Press these loops closed with needle-nose pliers (Figure 4).

Figure 5 shows the finished toggle bar.

Use one of the oval jump rings (Figure 6) to connect the toggle bar to the last link of the piece (Figure 7). See the Jump Ring section on pages 12 to 14 for instructions on opening and closing jump rings. Attach the twisted toggle jump ring to the other end of the piece with the other oval jump ring.

Place the toggle bar through the toggle ring sideways. The toggle bar should be just short enough to go through the toggle ring to make a secure fit. If the toggle ring is too large, or the toggle bar is too small, the piece will fall apart easily. Note the good fit in Figures 8 and 9.

Figure 6. Use a small, oval jump ring to connect the bar.

Figure 7. Toggle bar connected.

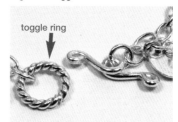

Figure 8. Note the size of the toggle ring compared to the size of the toggle bar.

Figure 9. Finished toggle clasp. A good fit.

15

S-Clasps

Materials

- 16-gauge (1.29 mm) dead soft wire
- 22-gauge (0.644 mm) dead soft wire
- 16-gauge ¼" (6 mm) diameter jump ring

Tools

- Ruler
- Flush or wire cutters
- Jeweler's flat file
- Felt-tipped pen (such as a Sharpie)
- Round-nose pliers
- Needle-nose pliers

Using the S-clasp is a simple but elegant way to finish off a necklace or bracelet. We've wrapped wire around the middle for embellishment. Another possibility would be to center a bead on the clasp with wraps on either side.

With a ruler, measure a 1¾" (4.5 cm) piece of 16-gauge (1.29 mm) wire and cut it with the flush cutters. Smooth the ends with the jeweler's flat file. This wire will be the clasp.

Measure and cut a 2" (5 cm) piece of 22-gauge (0.644 mm) wire with the flush cutters. Smooth the ends with the jeweler's flat file. This wire will be the wrapped embellishment (Figure 1).

Figure 1. The 22-gauge (0.644 mm) wire.

You can purchase S-clasps at hobby and bead stores, but it's less expensive to make your own. Check the clasps available for sale—some are very ornate and will give you ideas for personalizing your own.

Figure 2. Bend the 22-gauge (0.644 mm) wire in half with round-nose pliers.

Figure 3. Top wire to the right, bottom wire to the left.

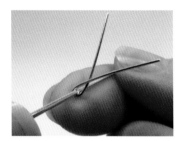

Figure 4. Slide the loop on the 16-gauge (1.29 mm) wire.

Figure 5. Begin wrapping.

Measure and mark with a felt-tipped pen the 22-gauge (0.644 mm) wire piece at the halfway mark. Use the very tip of the round-nose pliers to bend the wire in half (Figure 2).

Slant the top wire to the right and the bottom wire to the left. Doing so will facilitate starting the wrap (Figure 3).

Measure and mark the midpoint on the 16-gauge (1.29 mm) wire with the felt-tipped pen. Slide the 22-gauge (0.644 mm) wire loop to this point (Figure 4).

Begin to wrap by bringing the 22-gauge (0.644 mm) wire ends farther across to tighten them against the 16-gauge (1.29 mm) wire (Figures 5 and 6).

Support the wires against your index finger as shown in Figure 7.

Make one complete wrap with the top wire and then one complete wrap with the bottom wire (Figure 8).

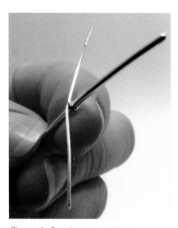

Figure 6. Continue wrapping.

Figure 7. Support the wires.

Figure 8. One wrap with top wire, then one wrap with bottom wire.

Getting Started Making Wire Jewelry

Figure 9. Complete about 6 wraps or ¼" (6 mm) worth of wraps.

Figure 10. Cut and file the ends. Press them into place.

Figure 11. Measure ⅜" (1 cm) and place in the middle of the round-nose pliers.

Complete about six wraps or ¼" (6 mm) worth of wraps (Figure 9).

Cut off the ends with the flush cutter, smooth them with the jeweler's flat file, and press the wires flat against the 16-gauge (1.29 mm) wire with needle-nose pliers. Be sure to press the wires down hard enough that the wrap will not move (Figure 10).

Measure ⅜" (1 cm) from the end of the wrap and mark the 16-gauge (1.29 mm) wire with the felt-tipped pen.

Place the wire in the middle of the round-nose pliers and make a curve toward the wrap (Figures 11 and 12).

Repeat the process on the other end of the clasp so that both end wires are even with the center wrappings (Figure 13).

Use needle- or round-nose pliers to bend the ends of the clasp slightly upward. Doing so will give the clasp a more finished look (Figure 14).

Figure 12. Make a curve toward the wrap.

Figure 13. Repeat the process on the other end.

Figure 14. Bend the ends of the clasp slightly upward.

Figure 15. Position round-nose pliers as shown.

Place one looped end of the piece inside one of the clasp ends. Position the round-nose pliers as shown in Figure 15.

While keeping the pliers against the areas shown, use a forward bending motion. Doing so will force the end down toward the wraps while you push up on the curve (Figure 16).

Use needle-nose pliers to press this end of the clasp completely closed. Doing so will prevent the bead loop from falling off and will further secure the wraps in the middle of the clasp.

Add a jump ring to the other end of the piece to provide a finished look.

The clasp end with which you open and close the piece should be very snug. Close this end of the clasp enough to first catch the jump ring and then snap it into place (Figure 17).

Figure 18 shows the finished clasp.

Figure 16. Pressing the loop closed.

Figure 17. Make the closure end very snug.

Figure 18. The finished S clasp.

Getting Started Making Wire Jewelry

Bangle Bracelet

Materials
- 16-gauge (1.29 mm) dead soft wire
- Charms or beads of your choice
- Jump rings of appropriate size for attaching charms or beads

Tools
- Ruler
- Flush or wire cutters
- Jeweler's flat file
- Rubber mallet
- Round-nose pliers
- Needle-nose pliers

This bangle is easy to make, and it does so many things! Some people love to hang all their childhood charms on it. Others add charms they've collected from around the world, still others use their children's birthstones. You can put Bali beads, stones, or just about anything on the bangle. Here's an idea: for a very special gift, personalize a bangle by adding alphabet beads to spell out a message or a name.

Use 16-gauge (1.29 mm) or larger round wire for this project. Sterling silver, gold-filled, copper, or brass are all suitable. With a ruler, measure a wire piece about 8½" (21.5 cm), cut it with the flush cutters, and smooth with the jeweler's flat file.

For a medium-size bracelet, about 7" (18 cm), you'll need a 2½" (6.5 cm) diameter circle. Form the wire around anything that is slightly smaller than 2½" (6.5 cm). The reason for doing this is that the wire will spring out larger than the object you form the wire around.

Figure 1. Wrap the metal wire around the mallet.

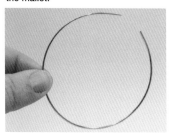

Figure 2. The finished circle.

Figure 3. Place the wire end in the largest part of the round-nose pliers.

Figure 4. Starting the P-loop.

We've used a 2" (5 cm) rubber mallet as a form. Wrap the wire around the mallet or whatever object you're using (Figure 1).

Figure 2 shows the finished circle. Choose one end for the catch.

Using round-nose pliers, make a large P-loop at the widest part of the pliers (Figures 3 and 4). Refer to Chapter 5 Connecting Beads, page 16, to review making P-loops. The P-loop should be oriented so that it lies flat against your wrist.

Figure 5 shows the P-loop still on the pliers.

Using needle-nose pliers, begin to center the P-loop by placing the pliers as shown in Figure 6.

Bend the loop back until it is centered over the rest of the wire (Figure 7). This loop will be the catch.

Now is a good time to add charms or other objects to the bangle using jump rings. You may also wait until the clasp is completed.

Next turn your attention to the other end of the circle. Grasp the wire with round-nose pliers about ¼" (6 mm) from the end of the pliers. Note that there's about ⅛" (3mm) of wire protruding from the pliers (Figure 8).

Figure 5. The P-loop formed in the round-nose pliers.

Figure 6. Beginning to center the P-loop.

Figure 7. The P-loop centered.

Figure 8. Starting the hook.

Getting Started Making Wire Jewelry

Figure 9. A different view of the bangle.

Figure 10. Complete the hook.

Figure 11. The hook end on top of the wire. The hook is too long to fit.

Hook end on top of wire

Figure 12. Cut off the end of the hook to shorten it.

Figure 9 shows a different view. You will be turning the hook back toward the bangle.

Complete the hook by rotating the round-nose pliers toward the bangle. (Figure 10).

Note that the hook end is bent up on top of the wire in Figure 11. We need to see if the hook will fit inside the loop. This hook is too long, but we can easily fix that.

To shorten the hook, use wire cutters to snip off just a little bit of wire. Keep snipping and trying the fit until the hook goes easily into the loop (Figures 12 and 13). File the newly cut end smooth with the jeweler's flat file.

Finish the bangle by pressing the loop down just enough for the hook to slide through easily (Figure 14). If you haven't already done so, you may now use jump rings to add charms or other objects to the bangle.

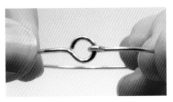

Figure 13. A good fit.

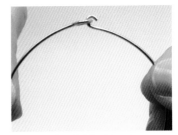

Figure 14. The finished bangle.

Bangle Bracelet

Spiral Bracelet

This pretty bracelet can be made using the skills you've already learned, especially the coil technique on pages 28 to 29. The spirals make this bracelet reminiscent of jewelry from ancient Greece, and its ornate appearance makes it look much harder to make than it really is.

Materials
- 16-gauge (1.30 mm) dead soft round wire (we've used sterling silver, but gold-filled, copper, or brass wire will work, too)

Tools
- Ruler
- Flush or regular wire cutters
- Jeweler's flat file
- Round-nose pliers
- Needle-nose pliers
- Flat-nose pliers
- Felt-tipped marker (such as a Sharpie)
- Large file with texture (used for coarse removal of metal or wood and can be found at the hardware store)

Measure and cut a 12" (30.5 cm) length of 16-gauge wire. File the ends smooth with the jeweler's flat file.

Place one end of the wire about one-third of the way up from the ends of the round-nose pliers. Press your left index finger against the wire and the pliers and roll the pliers to begin a loop (Figure 1). After the loop is started, move it closer to the tip of the round-nose pliers and complete the loop.

Use needle-nose pliers to squeeze the loop closed and to make it smaller (Figure 2). If the wire slips to the side, use flat-nose pliers to press the loop back into place.

Figure 1. Place wire in round nosed pliers and begin a loop.

Figure 2. Move the loop closer to the tip of the pliers. Squeeze the loop closed.

Figure 3. Place the loop deep inside the pliers.

Figure 4. Use round-nose pliers to press the wires together.

Figure 5. Make two complete circles.

You will now proceed to make a coil, much like the one on pages 28 to 29. Place the loop deep inside the flat-nose pliers and use your thumb to push the wire around the loop (Figure 3). If the second wrap becomes separated from the adjoining loop, use round-nose pliers to press the wires together as in Figure 4.

Continue to press the wire around until you have two complete circles (Figure 5).

Grasp the wire next to the completed circle with flat-nose pliers (Figure 6). Observe exactly where you place the wire on the pliers, as you will want to use the same spot for each link of the bracelet. It's a good idea to mark this spot with a felt-tipped marker. Using the inner circle as a guide, push the wire around the pliers to the other side of the spiral, forming a triangle (Figure 7).

Lay the flat-nose pliers across the entire spiral and bend the ending wire straight. Bend the ending wire toward the bottom of the spiral (Figure 8). If necessary, flatten the bracelet segment so that the swirls and triangle are all on the same plane.

Place the flat-nose pliers on the outer wire so they line up with the triangle and the inner loop. Turn the pliers and bend the wire until the wire is straight out at a 90° angle (Figure 9).

Figure 6. Grasp the wire with flat-nose pliers.

Figure 7. Push the wire to the other side of the spiral.

Figure 8. Bend the ending wire toward the bottom of the spiral.

Figure 9. Position the flat-nose pliers on the wire. Turn the wire out at a 90° angle.

Spiral Bracelet

Figure 10. The straight wire should be in line with the rest of the segment.

Figure 11. Cut the wire at the ⅜" (1 cm) mark.

Figure 12. File the end smooth.

Figure 13. Place the link on a metal surface and tap the spiral end with a hammer. Give the straight end a few extra taps to flatten it.

Figure 10 shows how the wire should align with the rest of the link.

Measure and mark the straight wire ⅜" (1 cm) from the turn. With the flat end of the wire cutters facing the spiral, cut the wire at the ⅜" (1 cm) mark (Figure 11) and file the end smooth with the jeweler's flat file (Figure 12).

To strengthen the piece, place it on a metal surface and tap it with a hammer to work-harden it. Hammer the spiral first, then hammer the rest of the wire (Figure 13). Just tap, tap, tap. You don't have to beat the poor link to death! You'll be able to feel the difference in the temper after a few taps. Give the end of the wire a few extra taps to flatten it slightly. This will make joining the links easier.

If you would like to add texture to your link, use a large file that has a pattern. Lay the file on the link and hit the file with a hammer (Figure 14). Turn the file in a different direction on the link and hammer the file again.

Figure 15 shows that the hammering has caused the outside wire to separate from the rest of the coil.

To get the wire back against the spiral, hold it with flat-nose pliers and grasp the end with your other hand. Press the wire behind the spiral, and then

Figure 14. To add texture, lay a large file on the link and hit it wih a hammer.

Figure 15. The wire has separated from the rest of the spiral.

Figure 16. Press the wire behind the spiral, then in front of the spiral.

Figure 17. Begin a loop.

Getting Started Making Wire Jewelry

Figure 18. The loop will be joined to the triangular part of another link.

press it in front of the spiral (Figure 16). Place the flat-nose pliers across the link and press everything flat again. These are the same steps we use to close a jump ring (see page 14).

Once the link is straightened, we'll make a loop at the end. Use round-nose pliers to grasp the end of the wire. As before, start the loop about one-third of the way up the pliers (Figure 17), and finish the loop by moving it close to the tip of the pliers. Curl the wire toward the back, nontextured side of the loop. Close the loop as before.

It probably won't surprise you to know that you're going to have to make more than one spiral link! Our links measure about ½" (1.3 cm) in length. The average female wrist is between 6½" (16.5 cm) and 7" (18 cm) in circumference—this will also be about the length of your bracelet. Of course, you'll want to add some wiggle room for the bracelet to fit somewhat loosely. The average bracelet is 7" (18 cm) long, so make about 12 more spiral links for now. We'll make the final link a little later—this last one will be the clasp.

We're going to join the loop of one link to the triangular part of another link (Figure 18).

Closing a loop and then re-opening it may seem silly, but doing this will help the wire remember where it's supposed to go and makes re-closing the loop a little easier.

Open a loop and join it to another link using the jump ring technique on page 14. Close the loop with needle-nose pliers. With the pliers positioned as in Figure 19, squeeze gently until the loop meets the wire.

Reposition the pliers and press gently again to make the loop rounder.

Figure 19. Joining one link to another and closing the loop.

Figure 20. Reposition the pliers to make the loop rounder.

Spiral Bracelet

Figure 21. Use round-nose pliers to grasp the wire.

Figure 22. Press the wire over the pliers.

Figure 23. The clasp should be in line with the rest of the link. This one needs work.

To make the clasp, make a spiral link as before, but leave the wire end ½" (1.3 cm) long. Use round-nose pliers to grasp the wire as shown in Figure 21. Don't forget to file the end smooth—this is your last chance!

Support the link with your index finger and press the wire over the pliers with your thumb (Figure 22).

Use the very tip of the round-nose pliers to make a little loop at the end of the wire. During all this curving and forming, the clasp will become a bit deformed. Figure 23 shows that the clasp is no longer in line with the rest of the link.

Use flat-nose pliers to hold the clasp and realign it with the rest of the link (Figure 24).

Place needle-nose pliers on either side of the end loop and squeeze the loop closed and into an oval shape (Figure 25). This will prevent the clasp from rubbing against or irritating the wrist when worn.

Place one jaw of the round-nose pliers inside the loop nearest the spiral and use your fingers to squeeze the clasp together (Figure 26). This should form a pleasing, gentle curve.

Figure 27 shows the finished clasp link.

Figure 24. Realign the clasp with the rest of the link.

Figure 25. Squeeze the end loop closed.

Figure 26. Use round-nose pliers to make a gentle curve.

Figure 27. The finished clasp link.

Getting Started Making Wire Jewelry

Try joining the clasp to the last link of the bracelet. The fit should be snug, with a little resistance and a snapping sound when the clasp is properly fitted (Figure 28).

When the bracelet is loose, the clasp will lay to the side as in Figure 29.

Figure 30 shows a bracelet with texture on every other link. You can also see that every other link is joined from either the bottom or the top. This is an excellent way to make the bracelet. If you decide to try this, you'll have to pay close attention while adding texture and joining the links.

Figure 31 shows a pair of matching earrings that use a plain head pin and "quad" Bali beads on either side of a gemstone; they attach to the spirals with wrapped bead loops (see page 21). Note that the spirals are mirror images of each other, so there is a right earring and a left earring. Simple loops attach to French ear wires.

We hope you enjoy making this simple but elegant bracelet and matching earrings!

Figure 28. Trying the clasp for proper fit.

Figure 29. The clasp will lay to the side when the bracelet is loose.

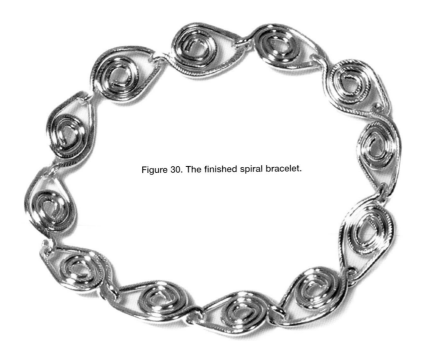

Figure 30. The finished spiral bracelet.

Figure 31. Matching earrings.

18

Chandelier Earrings

Chandelier earrings are sexy and fun and—you guessed it—easy to make! We're giving you one example of chandelier earrings. Once you know how to make this pair, you'll come up with lots of different designs. These earrings sell like crazy at jewelry shows and craft fairs, and everyone seems to think they must be difficult to make. Let's not let them in on our little secret, okay?

Materials

- 20-gauge (0.812 mm) dead soft silver wire
- 6 briolettes, 8x6mm
- 6 purchased oval jump rings, 3.6x2.7 mm, 19-gauge (you could make your own, but purchasing them in this size is much easier)
- 2 French ear wires, purchased or hand-made

Tools

- Ruler
- Flush or wire cutters
- Felt-tipped marker (such as a Sharpie)
- Round-nose pliers
- Needle-nose pliers

With a ruler, measure two pieces of 20-gauge (0.812 mm) dead soft silver wire 4" (10 cm) long and cut with the flush cutters.

Mark the midpoint of each wire with the felt-tipped pen and use round-nose pliers to make a pair of Us (Figure 1). To get the earrings to match, you must make each bend on both wires and match them up as you go. Be sure to mark the pliers about one quarter of the way from the end and use the same spot on the pliers for each bend.

Figure 1. Two wires bent in half.

Figure 2. Measure up ½" (1.3 cm) and mark. (This ruler is ½" (1.3 cm) wide.)

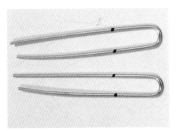

Figure 3. The marked wires.

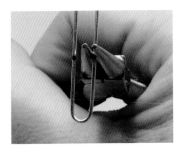

Figure 4. Round-nose pliers on a mark.

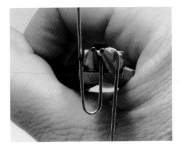

Figure 5. Second curve finished.

Lay the pieces beside each other and mark all four wires ½" (1.3 cm) up from the U with a felt-tip marker (Figures 2 and 3).

Place the round-nose pliers on a mark and bend the wire over the pliers with your index finger (Figures 4 and 5).

Repeat this process with the second wire and lay one wire on top of the other to make sure they match.

Repeat the bending process on the opposite side of the first U so that you have a piece that looks like Figure 6. Do the same with the second wire, then line it up and match it with the first. Do so with each curve in each wire.

Figure 7 shows how both wires should look at this point.

Line up the wires evenly and mark them ⅜" (1 cm) from the U ends (Figures 8 and 9).

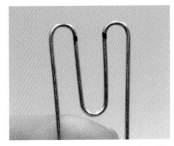

Figure 6. Original U in the middle with one curve on each side.

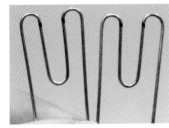

Figure 7. The wires should match.

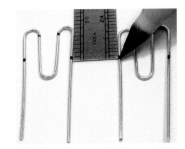

Figure 8. Measure ⅜" (1 cm) from the U.

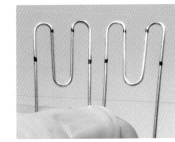

Figure 9. Both wires marked ⅜" (1 cm) from the top of the U.

Chandelier Earrings

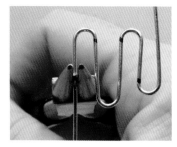

Figure 10. Preparing to make the next curve.

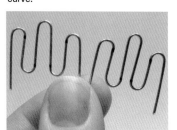

Figure 11. Both wires are finished.

Figure 12. Press the loops together.

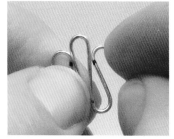

Figure 13. Use your fingers to press the wires closer together.

In Figure 10, we've already bent the right side up. For the left side, place the round-nose pliers on the marked wire. Use your index finger to bend the wire around the pliers until it looks like the right side.

Figure 11 shows both wires finished.

Use needle- or round-nose pliers to press the loops together (Figure 12).

If necessary, use your fingers to press the wires closer together (Figure 13).

If the wires still don't touch, press them a little past each other, then bend them back until they touch (Figure 14).

Figure 15 shows the two finished, matching wires.

Measure and mark ⅜" (1 cm) from each U on the end wires; cut (Figure 16).

Place the round-nose pliers on the very end of the wire (Figure 17). Roll the pliers down to create a loop.

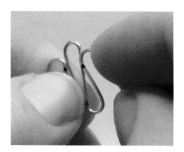

Figure 14. If necessary, press the wires past each other.

Figure 15. Matching wires, cut ⅜" (1 cm) from the U.

Figure 16. Round-nose pliers on the very end of the wire.

Figure 17. Make a loop.

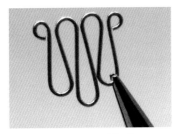

Figure 18. Make a matching loop on the other side.

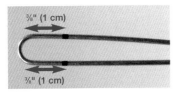

Figure 19. Make two U shapes and mark as indicated.

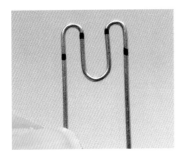

Figure 20. The first two bends completed and marked.

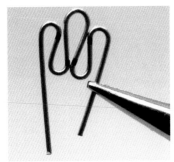

Figure 21. Loops made, end wires uneven.

Repeat on the other side (Figure 18). These wires will be the bottom part of the chandelier earrings.

Now we'll make the pieces for the tops of the earrings. Cut two pieces of wire 3" (7.5 cm) long and make a U in each as you did before. Measure and mark both sides of both pieces ⅜" (1 cm) from the top of the U (Figure 19).

Make the loops as you did with the first pieces. Measure and mark ⅜" (1 cm) from the tops of the U shapes on both wire pieces (Figure 20).

Make the next curves as shown in Figure 21. Press the curves together as before. Figure 21 shows that the wires are uneven.

Measure and cut off the longer wire so that the wire ends are even as in Figure 22.

Use the widest part of the round-nose pliers to make two large loops in each wire end. Join a top piece to a bottom piece by using oval jump rings through the loops.

Figure 23 shows the two wire components joined by oval jump rings.

It's a good idea to attach the ear wires to the earrings now. Doing so will help you visualize the front and back of the earrings and how well the wires

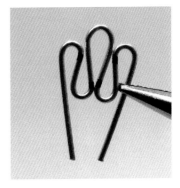

Figure 22. Wires have been cut to the same length.

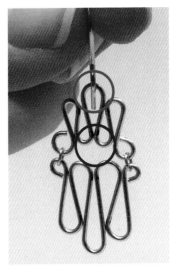

Figure 23. Top and bottom components joined by oval jump rings.

Figure 24. Put the first bead on the middle earring loop.

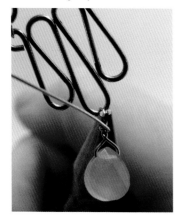

Figure 25. Wrap down over the twists.

Figure 26. The first stone finished.

are hanging. Refer to the jump-ring chapter page 14 for opening and closing techniques. Use an oval jump ring to attach the ear wire to the middle U in the top component of each earring (see the red circle in Figure 23).

We've chosen briolettes for this project, but you can use any stone of any color, natural or man-made. Whatever suits your personal taste. You can also add beads to the curves in the top wire component (see the blue circle in Figure 23). Now we'll attach the briolettes to the bottom wire components to finish the earrings. Please refer to the chapter on briolettes for instructions on wrapping them (pages 39 to 42).

Make the twists and start the loop. Put the loop through the middle curve in the bottom wire component and wrap (Figures 24 and 25). Hold both sides of the loop with needle-nose pliers while you wrap.

Figure 26 shows the first briolette finished.

Repeat the process to the right of the center loop (Figure 27).

For the left curve, bring the stone in from the back of the earring (Figure 28). Doing so will make the right and left stones mirror images of each other.

Figure 29 shows a finished earring.

Figure 27. Middle and right stones in place.

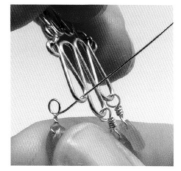

Figure 28. Bring the third stone in from the back of the earrings.

Figure 29. Finished!

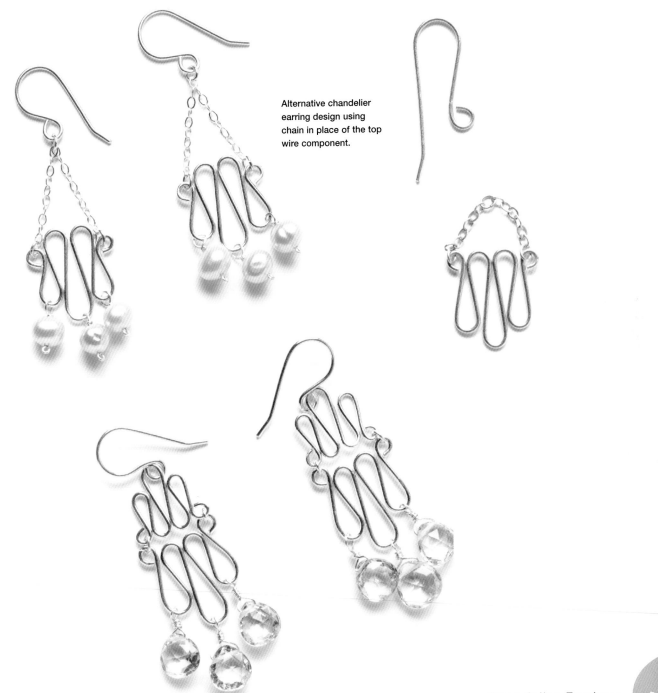

Alternative chandelier earring design using chain in place of the top wire component.

19

Knot Rings

Linda has sentimental feelings about this ring, which is also called a Lover's Knot Ring—her father gave one to her mother before they were married. Historically, a knot ring can be made of ribbon or other material, and it symbolizes love and commitment. It's also simply a cute little ring that can be worn on any finger—or toe.

Materials

- 18- or 20-gauge (1.02 or 0.812 mm) dead soft wire

Tools

- Ruler
- Flush or wire cutters
- Wooden ring mandrel with grooves
- Masking tape
- Needle-nose pliers
- Jeweler's flat file

With the ruler, measure about 8" (20.5 cm) of wire and cut it with the wire cutters. We'll wrap the wire around the ring mandrel just as we wrapped wire around a dowel to make jump rings (see page 13).

Figure 1. Place the middle of the wire on size seven of the ring mandrel.

Figure 2. Make two tight wraps.

Figure 3. Remove the ring from the mandrel.

Figure 4. Wrap masking tape around the back of the ring.

tart in the middle of the wire and use your fingers to wrap from both sides. We've started at size seven (Figure 1). Make two tight wraps around the mandrel, wrapping from both ends of the wire (Figure 2).

Have a piece of masking tape ready. When you are satisfied that the loops are straight on the mandrel, and tight, remove the loops from the mandrel very carefully to maintain their shape and tightness (Figure 3).

Holding the crossed wires, wrap masking tape around the back of the ring (Figure 4).

The ring should look like Figure 5 at this point.

Now place the ring back on the mandrel, still holding the wire crossing tightly (Figure 6).

Keeping your thumb firmly pressed against the wire crossing, pull the left wire (B) down and across the other wires. Pull the right wire (A) up and across the other wires. Your ring should now look like Figure 7. Remove the ring from the mandrel.

Use needle-nose pliers to hold the end of the right wire (A). Guide the wire behind all the other wires (Figure 8).

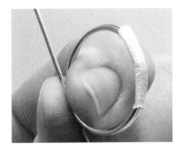

Figure 5. Ring with masking tape.

Figure 6. Place the ring back on the mandrel.

Figure 7. Left wire down (B), right wire up (A).

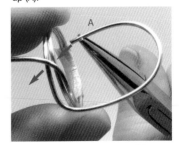

Figure 8. Guide the right wire (A) behind all the other wires.

Knot Rings

Figure 9. Use needle-nose pliers to help form a loop.

Figure 10. Further define the loop.

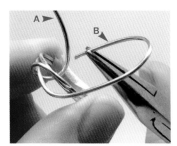

Figure 11. Bring the left wire (B) behind the other wires.

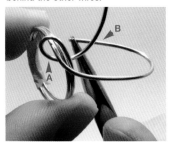

Figure 12. Placing the left wire (B) inside the loop.

Move the needle-nose pliers closer to the loop you are now forming from the right wire (A). Use a very light touch to feed the wire (A) farther behind the other wires until it has a definite loop shape (Figure 9).

Further define the loop by using the needle-nose pliers to shape a loop with a small opening (Figure 10).

Turn the ring upside down. Use the needle-nose pliers to grasp the very end of the left wire (B) and guide it around and down behind the other wires as you did with the right wire (A) (Figure 11). Don't give up, this process *will* make sense! Put the left wire (B) inside the loop formed with the right wire (A). See the notations and arrow in Figure 12.

As shown in Figure 13, begin to guide the left wire (B) through the loop made by the right wire (A).

Keep working with the left wire (B), pushing and pulling the wire through the loop. Use a light touch with the pliers to avoid marring the metal (Figure 14).

Finally! This knot is beginning to take shape! Keep pushing and pulling until your knot looks like the one in Figure 15.

Tighten the loops as much as possible by pushing, pulling, and squeezing (Figure 16).

Figure 13. Bring the left wire (B) through the loop.

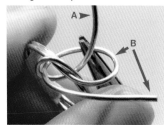

Figure 14. Keep pushing and pulling the wire through the loop.

Figure 15. Keep pushing and pulling until your knot looks like this.

Figure 16. Tighten the loops.

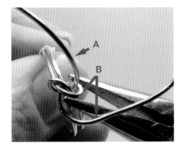

Figure 17. Tighten further.

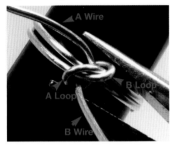

Figure 18. Press the wires firmly against the loops.

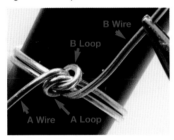

Figure 19. Bring the wires close to their loops.

Figure 20. Wires close to their loops.

Figure 17 shows the loops tightened even more. Slide the ring onto the ring mandrel and place the knot in the groove.

Now we need to deal with the loose wires. Use needle-nose pliers to press the wires down on either side of the knot as far as possible (Figure 18).

Bend the A wire down to lie against the first A loop. Bring the B wire up to lie against the B loop (Figures 19 and 20).

Things are definitely looking better, don't you think?

Remove the ring from the mandrel and continue to press the wires down with needle-nose pliers (Figure 21).

Still using needle-nose pliers, grasp the end of one wire and bring it around to the back of the ring (Figures 22 and 23). Just follow the wire next to the one you're working with now.

Repeat the same process with the other wire and loop. Press the remaining wires flat against the inside of the ring (Figure 24).

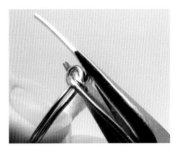

Figure 21. Continue to press the wires down.

Figure 22. Grasp the end of one wire.

Figure 23. Bring the wire around, down, and through the loop.

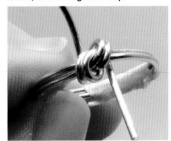

Figure 24. Press the wires against the inside of the ring.

Figure 25. The inside of the ring with the wires pressed down.

Figure 26. The inside of the ring showing the cut wires.

Figure 27. The finished ring.

Figure 25 shows the inside of the ring with the wires pressed tightly into place.

Still using the needle-nose pliers, pull each wire up just enough to cut the end with the flush cutters. Cut the wire so that it will lie halfway across the back of the band (Figure 26). File the end smooth with the jeweler's flat file and press back in place with the needle-nose pliers.

Note that we pressed the wire down and then lifted it up to cut it, which sounds a little crazy. However, this process makes the wire go back into place much easier.

Once you master this ring, you can make the larger, more complex rings shown in Figure 28.

Figure 28. More complex knot rings.

Finished earring with the toggle bar toward the front.

Toggle Earrings

20

Materials

- About 12" (30.5 cm) of 1.4 mm cable chain (This is plain chain from which you might hang a pendant or charm, and it is available in hobby stores and jewelry-supply catalogs.)
- Eight 4mm iolite rondels (Rondels are donut-shaped stones that can be purchased at hobby and jewelry supply stores.)
- Eight 4x6mm oval pearls
- 8 head pins, 22- or 24-gauge
- 4 purchased or handmade 21-gauge ³⁄₁₆" (5 mm) diameter round jump rings
- 2 purchased mini toggle clasps—the jump ring is ⁵⁄₁₆" (9 mm) in diameter and the bar is ½" (1.3 cm) long
- 2 French ear wires, purchased or hand-made

Tools

- Flush or wire cutters
- Round-nose pliers
- Needle-nose pliers
- Flat-nose pliers

Several cascades can provide many looks for one pair of toggle earrings. Just remove the bar that the cascade hangs on and replace it with a bar of different stones! These elegant and versatile earrings can also be worn without the toggle—simply attach the jump ring of the pearl cascade to an ear wire instead of a toggle.

Figure 1 shows the components we'll be using for these earrings.

For the cascading effect, use the wire cutters to cut the chain in four lengths as follows: three links, six links, twelve links, and sixteen links, labeled in Figure 2.

Add an iolite rondel and an oval pearl to each head pin. Use round-nose pliers to make a wrapped bead loop at the top of the pearl as described on pages 21 to 23 of Chapter 5, Connecting Beads (Figure 3); thread the head pin through a link at one end of a length of chain.

Figure 1. Components for the earrings.

Figure 2. Number of links per chain.

Figure 3. Wrapped bead loop on chain.

Figure 4. Thread the last link of chain onto the jump ring.

Use needle- and flat-nose pliers to open a jump ring; thread the last chain onto the jump ring. Refer to the Jump Rings section on page 14 for instructions on opening and closing jump rings. Leave the jump ring open (Figure 4).

Repeat this process on the three remaining lengths of chain; thread them onto the jump ring. Now thread a toggle bar onto the jump ring (Figure 5).

Close the jump ring. Figure 6 shows how the earring should look at this point.

Add another jump ring to the circle part of a toggle clasp. Thread the toggle bar through the toggle circle. Leave the upper jump ring open (Figure 7).

Add an ear wire to the top jump ring and close the jump ring. The toggle bar should face toward the front of the earring.

When you make the second earring, reverse the order in which you place the chains on the jump ring. Thus, in the second earring, the lengths of chain will go, from left to right, six links, sixteen links, twelve links, and three links. This pattern will improve the earrings' appearance by making them mirror images when worn.

Figure 5. Thread the toggle bar onto the jump ring.

Figure 6. Close the jump ring.

Figure 7. Toggle clasp joined. Top jump ring added.

Bead and Pearl Bracelet

21

Materials

- 20-gauge (0.812mm) dead soft wire
- 26-gauge (0.405mm) dead soft wire or 26-gauge head pins
- 8mm round beads (we've used onyx) The number of beads required will depend on the width of the bracelet. Ten is a good number to try. A bead can always be added or subtracted.
- 4x6mm oval freshwater pearls, or beads or charms of your choice, 8 for each round bead, above
- 18 gauge, purchased ¼" (6mm) diameter jump rings
- Bead caps. We've used silver Bali bead caps, which are available at hobby stores. Each bead takes two caps. They're not necessary, but they're pretty!

Tools

- Needle-nose pliers
- Wire cutters
- Round-nose pliers
- Flat-nose pliers

This lovely bracelet combines several techniques you've learned in previous chapters. It is a joy to wear or give. Remember that the materials listed are guidelines. Now that you've gained some proficiency in jewelry making, feel free to alter the materials to suit your taste. And please don't forget to have fun!

Figure 1. Beads with plain bead loops.

Figure 2. Components for the bracelets.

Figure 3. Add a pearl to the bead loop.

The beads in Figure 1 are strung together with plain bead loops, as discussed earlier in the book (see pages 16 and 17).

Figure 2 shows the beads and some freshwater pearls that have been embellished with the swirl you also learned to make earlier in the book (see pages 44 to 42). There is also a jump ring strung with four pearls. We'll get to that jump ring a little later.

Make all the beads with loops—see pages 15 to 18 of the Connecting Beads section for instructions. The looped beads may be made with or without bead caps. Make all the pearls with swirls—see the Swirl Bead section on pages 44 to 46 for instructions.

Open a bead loop with needle-nose pliers and place one pearl in the loop (Figure 3).

Add another pearl and close the bead loop (Figure 4).

Open one loop of another bead with loops. Add two pearls to the loop and join the open loop to the closed loop you just worked on (Figure 5).

Close the bead loop. You now have two beads with two pearls on each that are joined together (Figure 6).

Figure 4. Add another pearl and close the bead loop.

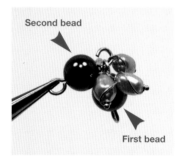

Figure 5. Second bead loop with two pearls and first bead with loop.

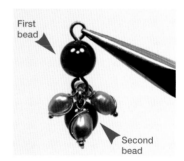

Figure 6. Close the second bead loop.

Getting Started Making Wire Jewelry

Figure 7. Another view of the two joined beads.

Figure 8. Beads with wrapped bead loops.

Figure 9. Pearls on jump rings.

Things may seem a bit crowded, but you'll master this technique in a jiffy!

Figure 7 shows another view of the two joined beads. Now you will simply open one of the closed bead loops, add two pearls, and close the loop. Then take a third plain bead with loops, open one loop, add two more pearls, join it to the second closed loop, and close the loop. Continue adding beads and pearls until you've reached the length you want for the bracelet. Finish off the bracelet with one of the clasps in this book (we suggest a toggle clasp) and wear with pride!

Here's another option for a slightly different look. If you wish, make wrapped bead loops (Figure 8). But of course, you can't open and close them!

For yet another effect, add jump rings with pearls in between the beads—the pearls will move freely around on their jump rings and hang gracefully (Figure 9).

Figure 10 shows a finished bracelet before a clasp is added.

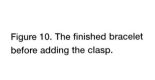

Figure 10. The finished bracelet before adding the clasp.

Bead and Pearl Bracelet

22

Inexpensive 6mm beads from your bead or hobby shop.

Wire Embellished Greeting Cards

Here's a little something fun you can create with your newly gained knowledge of jewelry making! Commercial greeting cards that are embellished with wire are expensive, but not these! Give them to friends and relatives—but keep all the fun of making them for yourself.

There are no rules, and the only limitation is your own imagination. We're going to explain how to make one card to get your creative juices flowing. We hope you enjoy making these very special cards!

Your local hobby store will usually have an aisle devoted to scrapbooking. This is where you'll find the special papers that are used in this project. A trip to the jewelry-making aisle should turn up lots of charms, seed beads, and other materials to incorporate into your card. This aisle is also where you're most likely to find colored copper wire in various gauges. Our card uses 32-gauge beading wire throughout, but please feel free to experiment with other colors and gauges.

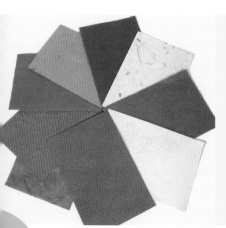

Materials
- Card stock
- Handmade paper
- 32-gauge gold-colored beading wire (we've used Fun Wire®)
- Fifteen 6mm seed beads (we've used "opaque rainbow" beads)
- Sewing thread that matches the wire color

Tools
- Scissors
- Ruler
- Pencil
- Flat-nose pliers
- Sewing needle
- Double-sided tape

Figure 1. Tear the paper along the side of the ruler.

Figure 2. Use a pencil to form a loop in the middle of each wire.

Figure 3. String three 6mm beads onto a wire.

Figure 4. Twisting the wires to form a stem.

Cut a piece of card stock about 8½ x 5½" (14 x 21.5 cm) and fold in half to make a card.

The handmade paper for the front of the card should be about 3 x 4½" (7.5 x 11.5 cm). Measure and mark the back side of this paper with ruler and pencil. (The back side is smoother than the front.)

Place the ruler on the marks and tear the paper along the side of the ruler (Figure 1).

For the bead bouquet, cut five pieces of beading wire about eight inches long. Fold each wire in half, using a pencil to form a loop in the middle (Figure 2).

String three 6mm beads onto a wire (Figure 3). Push the beads together in the middle of the loop. Using flat-nose pliers, twist the wires snugly against the beads and into a long stem (Figures 4 though 6).

Repeat the process with the other four wires.

You should have five stems about 4" (10 cm) long, with three beads at the top (Figure 7).

Starting about 2" (5 cm) down from the beads, twist the stems together into a trunk (Figure 8).

Figure 5. Wire snug against beads.

Figure 6. Completed stem.

Figure 7. Five stems.

Figure 8. Twist the stems together into a trunk.

Wire Embellished Greeting Cards

Figure 9. Position bouquet on paper.

Figure 10. Bring the needle and thread up through the paper to the front.

Figure 11. Pulling thread up.

Position the wire and bead bouquet on the front side of the handmade paper (Figure 9).

Attach the bouquet to the paper with needle and thread. Starting at either side of the beads and leaving a tail long enough to tie a knot, bring the needle and thread up through the back of the paper, on the outside edge of a bead flower, and then down on the inside of the flower to the back side of the paper (Figures 10 through 12).

Tie the working thread to the tail.

Without cutting the thread, continue on to the next flower and repeat until all the flowers are anchored to the paper.

Now repeat the process at one or two places on the trunk of the bouquet. Knot the thread on the back of the paper to secure it (Figure 13).

Place several pieces of double-sided tape on the back of the paper (Figure 14).

Figure 12. Needle and thread go back down inside the flower to the back side of the paper.

Figure 13. Back side of paper, showing thread.

Figure 14. Place double-sided tape on the back of the paper.

Center the paper on the card stock and press firmly into place (Figure 15).

You're finished!

Figure 16 shows a variation on the bouquet, using different paper.

Figure 17 shows another idea for a card. This card was made with 4mm pink fire-polished beads, a vintage crystal for the ring, and 24-gauge wire.

Figure 15. Center the paper onto the card and press firmly into place.

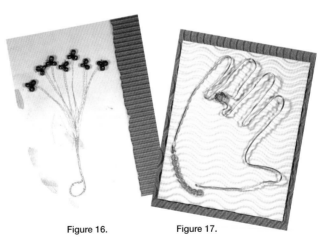

Figure 16.

Figure 17.

Resources

SUPPLIES

FDJ Tools
(407) 629-6906
(800) 323-6091 Telephone orders
(407) 645-0707 Fax
(800) 634-1070 Fax orders
1180 Solana Ave.
Winterpark, FL 32789
www.fdjtool.com
Specialties: Tools, equipment, and displays

Fire Mountain Gems & Beads
(800) 355-2137 Telephone orders
(800) 423-2319 Customer service
(800) 292-3473 Fax
One Firemountain Wy.
Grant's Pass, OR 97526-2373
www.firemountaingems.com
Specialties: Beads, gems, and beading supplies

Hoover & Strong
(800) 759-9997
10700 Trade Rd.
Richmond, VA 23236-3000
www.hooverandstrong.com
Specialties: Colored gold (white, green, pink), Surgical steel body jewelry, settings, and refining

Indian Jewelers Supply Company
(800) 545-6540
(888) 722-4175 Fax
601 East Coal Ave.
Gallup, NM 87301
www.ijsinc.com
orders@ijsinc.com
catalogs@ijsinc.com
Specialties: Tools, equipment, materials, and findings

Otto Frei
(510) 823-0355
(800) 900-3734 Fax
(510) 832-0355 International telephone
(510) 834-6217 International fax
PO Box 796
126 Second St.
Oakland, CA 94604
www.ofrei.com
Specialties: Tools and equipment

Rio Grande (The Bell Group)
(800) 545-6566
(800) 965-2329 Fax
(800) 253-9738 Telephone for Canada, Virgin Islands, and Puerto Rico
(505) 839-3011 Telephone for all other countries
(505) 839-3016 Fax for all other countries
7500 Bluewater Rd. Northwest
Albuquerque, NM 87121-1962
www.riogrande.com
Specialties: Tools and equipment, materials, display projects, and refining

Rishashay
(800) 517-3311
(406) 549-3467 Fax
PO Box 8271
Missoula, MT 59807
inquire@rishashay.com
Specialties: Bali beads, clasps, bead caps, and finished jewelry

WEBSITES

www.ganoksin.com
Lurk and learn as some of the most prominent people in the jewelry business discuss every aspect of jewelry making. When you feel brave enough, put your question(s) before this group of experts. Beginners' questions are answered clearly and generously. Ganoksin also has galleries of members' work as well as an extensive library of topics. Metalcalc can help you with any mathematical formulae or conversions.

www.jewelrymaking.about.com
This site has projects and technical information related to jewelry making.

www.lapidaryjournal.com
This is Lapidary Journal magazine's website with lots of projects and technical information.

BOOKS
McCreight, Tim. *The Complete Metalsmith.* New York: Sterling Publishing, 1991.

McGrath, Jinks. *The Encyclopedia of Jewelry Making Techniques.* Philadelphia: Running Press, 2003.

Wicks, Sylvia. *Jewelry Making Manual.* Edison, New Jersey: Chartwell House, 1989.

MAGAZINES

Art Jewelry
www.artjewelrymag.com

Bead & Button
www.beadandbutton.com

Beadwork
www.interweave.com/bead/default.asp

Lapidary Journal
www.lapidaryjournal.com

The Sunshine Artist
www.sunshineartist.com

Index

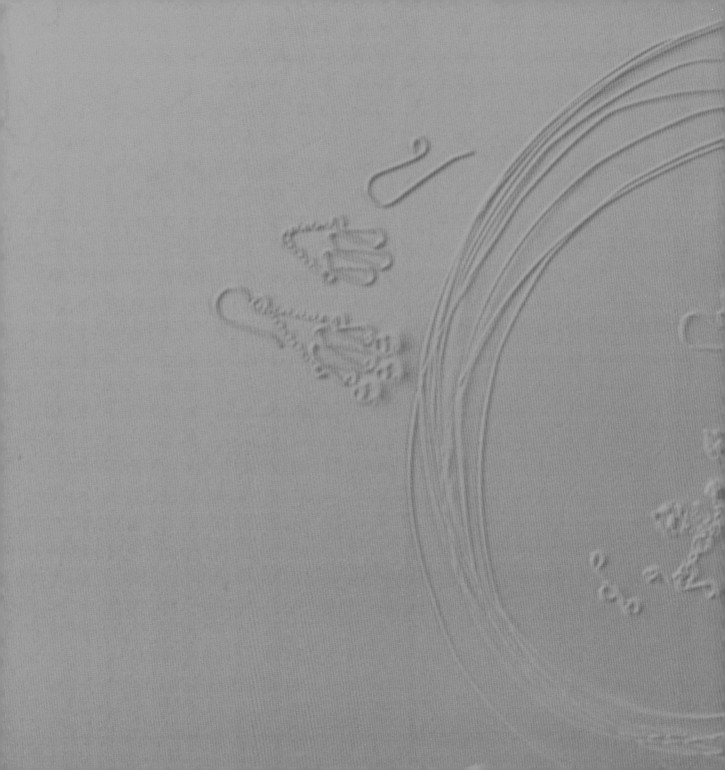